Hindi-English English-Hindi Dictionary & Phrasebook

Dictionary & Phrasebooks

Albanian
Arabic
Arabic (Eastern) *Romanized*
Australian
Azerbaijani
Basque
Bosnian
Breton
British
Cajun French
Chechen
Croatian
Czech
Danish
Dari *Romanized*
Esperanto
Estonian
Finnish
French
Georgian
German
Greek
Hebrew
Hungarian
Igbo
Ilocano
Irish
Italian
Japanese *Romanized*
Lao *Romanized*
Lingala
Malagasy
Maltese
Mongolian
Nepali *Romanized*
Norwegian
Pashto *Romanized*
Pilipino (Tagalog)
Polish
Québécois
Romanian
Romansch
Russian
Shona
Sicilian
Slovak
Somali
Spanish (Latin American)
Swahili
Swedish
Tajik
Thai *Romanized*
Turkish
Ukrainian
Urdu *Romanized*
Uzbek

Hindi-English
English-Hindi
Dictionary & Phrasebook

Todd Scudiere

Hippocrene Books, Inc.
New York

For information, address:
HIPPOCRENE BOOKS, INC.
171 Madison Avenue
New York, NY 10016

Book design and composition by Susan A. Alquist.

Library of Congress Cataloging-in-Publication Data

Scudiere, Todd.
Hindi-English/English-Hindi : dictionary & phrase book / Todd Scudiere.
p. cm.
ISBN 0-7818-0983-5
1. Hindi language--Dictionaries--English. 2. English language--Dictionaries--Hindi. 3. Hindi Language--Conversation and phrase books--English. 4. English language--Conversation and phrase books--Hindi. I. Title: English-Hindi. II. Title.

PK1936.S4436 2003
491.4'3321--dc22

2003056988

Printed in the United States of America.

Contents

Acknowledgments

I hope that this book is a rewarding and useful tool for travelers to India and students of Hindi. May it help to bridge communication and promote understanding between cultures.

I would like to thank my family and friends for all of their encouragement and support throughout the project. Special thanks to my friend Mona Maniar for her helpful suggestions and editing work.

This book is dedicated to my family, and to my second families in India, the Kumars of New Delhi and the Tripathis of Varanasi.

Introduction

Hindi is a beautiful language that is a joy both to learn and to speak. It is estimated to be the second or third most widely spoken language in the world. Hindi and its related dialects are spoken by an estimated 300 million people. One can find Hindi speakers not only in the North of India, but also in places such as Fiji, Mauritius, parts of the Middle East, and many other locations around the globe. Hindi speakers also can communicate fairly well in Urdu, the national language of Pakistan, which is spoken in many parts of India. While Urdu is similar to Hindi, a far greater number of its words are Perso-Arabic in origin. Also, while Hindi is written in the *Devanāgarī* script and is read left to right, Urdu is written in a version of the Arabic script and is read right to left. While both languages are almost identical in their sentence structure and share a wealth of vocabulary, they reflect individual cultural traditions. These languages tend to be separated by politics more than anything else. In reality, in many parts of North India such as Delhi, a combination of the two languages will be spoken, known as "Hindustānī."

This book is intended to offer an introduction to the modern standard Hindi that is spoken and taught in many parts of India and understood by many speakers of other related dialects. However, there are many commonly used words in Hindi of Perso-Arabic origin that, while "officially" considered to be "Urdu" words, are more widely used in colloquial Hindi than the Sanskrit-derived Hindi equivalents, and they have been included throughout this book. In the dictionary section, every attempt has been made to offer the most commonly used translation that will be of greatest benefit to the traveler.

All of the phrasebook and dictionary entries are given in English, romanized Hindi, and *Devanāgarī* script. For the Hindi-English section of the dictionary, the romanized Hindi has been given first and alphabetized according to English dictionary order to aid the traveler and beginning student.

Abbreviations

adj.	adjective
adv.	adverb
aux.	auxiliary
conj.	conjunction
f.	feminine
fam.	familiar
for.	formal
inf.	informal
int.	intimate
interj.	interjection
interr.	interrogative
lit.	literally
m.	masculine
n.	noun
phr.	phrase
pl.	plural
post.	postposition
prep.	preposition
pron.	pronoun
s.	singular
v.i.	intransitive verb
v.t.	transitive verb

Introduction to the *Devanāgarī* Script & Pronunciation Guide

Hindi is written in the *Devanāgarī* script. *Devanāgarī,* thousands of years old, is the same script used to write Sanskrit as well as Hindi, Marathi, Nepali, and other Indic languages and dialects that have their origins in Sanskrit. Many other languages use a variation of *Devanāgarī.*

In this book, every attempt has been made to use a consistent transcription system with only slight variations. For example, in certain cases, vowels are not pronounced. In order to enable you to pronounce the words as correctly as possible so that you will be understood, slight adjustments have been made in the transliterations of the phrases and words in the dictionary, where required. In some cases vowels have been dropped intentionally in the romanized word to insure proper pronunciation. Also, in general, the vowel *a* is not pronounced if it falls at the end of a word. If an "a" sound is to be pronounced, it will be written as a long *ā* instead.

EXAMPLE:

किताब
कि + ता + ब
ki + tā + ba = kitāb = book

Notice that the word is not pronounced *kitāba*. The final vowel is dropped. In Sanskrit, a symbol known as a *visarga* is placed after a letter when the final vowel is not to be pronounced. So, *kitāb* would be written *किताब्* instead of *किताब*. However, in Hindī this feature has been dropped. Another example is in the case of the pronoun *vah*, which will be transcribed in this book as *voh* as this is a more common pronunciation and you will be better understood. In addition, words ending in a *y* sound such as *cāy*, or "tea", are really pronounced as *cāi*. It is very important to learn the pronunciation of the diacritics well so that you can distinguish some of the subtle differences between aspirated, non-aspirated, retroflex, and other unique sounds in Hindi that will be discussed in detail in this chapter. The most common confusion with the transliteration might occur with the *ca* sound, which is really pronounced as *cha* with no aspiration, as in the final *ch* sound in the English word *chur**ch***. Therefore, *cāi* is to be pronounced *chai*. The "h" has been omitted in the transcription so as not to confuse it with *ch*, which is another Hindi letter that is aspirated.

Hindi is written from left to right, below a continuous line. This line does have breaks within a word as certain letters that are "open" on top require them (notice where the line falls over each individual letter in the consonant chart).

There are traditionally no periods used in Hindi. A sentence is ended with a single line, or *ḍaṇḍā* (*lit.* "pole") that looks like this: ।

Notice the *ḍaṇḍā* at the end of this sentence:

आप का नाम क्या है ।

Traditionally, paragraphs are ended with a double *ḍaṇḍā* as shown in this example:

आप का नाम क्या है ॥

Please note that the new practice is to use a period or "full stop" to end a sentence or paragraph, especially in magazines, newspapers, etc. As you will still see the *ḍaṇḍā* being used, it is best to be aware of it as well as the period or "full stop" that we use in English. As with English, many times there will be no period or *ḍaṇḍā* such as with signs such as "no smoking," etc. Exclamation points and question marks are also becoming commonly used in Hindi, although this is a recent development.

What follows is an alphabet chart, with romanized pronunciations and examples of similar sounds in English. The order in which these letters are given corresponds to the traditional Hindi dictionary order.

Hindi Vowels & Their Transliteration

अ *a*	short "a" sound as in b**u**s
आ *ā*	long "a" sound as in f**a**ther
इ *i*	short "i" sound as in p**i**n
ई *ī*	long "i" sound, pronounced like the "ee" in sl**ee**ve
उ *u*	short "u" sound as in p**u**t
ऊ *ū*	long "u" sound as in f**oo**l
ए *e*	sounds like the "a" sound in g**a**me or c**a**ke
ऐ *ai*	as in m**e**n but for some speakers in different regions it sounds like the "i" sound in sm**i**le
ओ *o*	as in m**o**st

औ

au as in c**ou**gh or sometimes stronger as in c**ou**ch or w**o**w

The following vowels only occur in Sanskrit loanwords and include the *r* consonant with either a short or long *i* sound:

ऋ

ri as in t**ri**ck

ॠ

rī as in **ree**f

Notes on Pronunciation

Aspirated Sounds

Aspirated sounds require a slight exhalation when they are pronounced. In this book, whenever you see an *h* immediately after a consonant, such as in the word *kharāb* ("bad"), you will know that this word requires a slight aspiration. When you practice saying aspirated sounds, hold your hand at a short distance from your mouth. You will feel a slight breath on your hand if you are saying these sounds correctly.

Retroflex Sounds

Retroflex sounds are formed by placing the tip of the tongue on the roof of the mouth. Hindi also has different types of "d" and "t" sounds that are often difficult for English speakers to reproduce. When you pronounce a retroflex sound, place the tip of your tongue on the roof of your mouth and voice the sound. When the sound is both retroflex and aspirated, follow the above instructions, but this time exhale slightly to produce a "ha" sound after the initial consonant. Most retroflex sounds have been romanized with a "." underneath the letter. When this sound is both retroflex and aspirated, an "h" will follow.

EXAMPLE:

त is the regular "t" in Hindi, transcribed as "ta"
ट is a non-aspirated, retroflex "t" in Hindi, transcribed as "ṭa"
ठ is the aspirated and retroflex "t" in Hindi, transcribed as "ṭha"

Dental Sounds

Dental sounds are formed by pressing the front edge of the tongue behind the teeth of the upper jaw. When aspirated, a slight breath should be heard. Here is an example:

त is the regular "t" sound transcribed as "ta." Place the tip of your tongue behind the front teeth of your upper jaw and say "ta" without aspirating.

थ is the aspirated version of the त above. Follow the same instructions as above, but this time exhale slightly to pronounce "tha."

Hindi Consonants & Their Transliteration

क

ka "k" sound as in s**k**irt

ख

kha "kh" sound as in **kh**aki

ग

ga "g" sound as in Sprin**g**

घ

gha "g" sound as in **g**um, but aspirated

ङ

ṅa "n" sound as in bli**n**k. To make this sound, roll the tip of your tongue quickly across the roof of your mouth while pronouncing *ṅa*. This will produce the required "flapping" sound unique to this letter.

च

ca non-aspirated "ch" sound as in ri**ch** or the final "ch" sound in chur**ch**

छ

cha aspirated "ch" sound as in **ch**arm or the initial "ch" sound in **ch**urch

ज

ja "j" sound as in brid**ge**

झ

jha "j" sound as in **j**ump, but aspirated

ञ

ña "n" sound as in i**n**jury

ट

ṭa "t" sound as in plan**t**, retroflex

ठ

ṭha same retroflex "t" sound as above, but aspirated, more like **t**able

ड

ḍa "d" sound as in blan**d**, retroflex

ढ

ḍha same retroflex "d" sound as above, but aspirated, more like **d**am

ण

ṇa same "n" sound as above, but retroflexed, more like **n**ine

ड़

ṛa is the retroflex version of ड (*ḍa*). This letter usually becomes *ṛa* when it falls in between two vowels. To make this sound, place the tip of your tongue on the roof of your mouth and say "da," flapping the tip of your tongue slightly.

ढ़
ṛha is the same as the above letter, but aspirated as well. Follow the above instructions for *ṛa*, and this time exhale slightly.

त
ta soft "t" sound as in the French word ver**t**e

थ
tha same "t" sound as above, but aspirated, more like **ta**lk

द
d "d" sound as in Concor**d**e

ध
dh same "d" sound as above, but aspirated, more like **d**onut

न
na "n" sound as in bea**n**

प
pa "p" sound as in cu**p**

फ
pha "ph" sound as in **p**arty, but aspirated

ब

ba "b" sound as in la**b**

भ

bha "b" sound as in **b**akery, but aspirated

म

ma "m" sound as in **m**other

य

ya "y" sound as in **y**ard

र

ra "r" sound as in **r**ap but rolled or trilled slightly

ल

la "l" sound as in **l**ove

व

va a combination of the "w" sound as in **w**ater and "v" sound as in lo**v**e

श

śa "sh" sound as in ca**sh** or **sh**opping

ष

ṣa "sh" sound as in ca**sh** but retroflexed (say with tip of tongue on roof of mouth)

स

sa "s" sound as in **s**oap

ह

ha "h" sound as in **h**ouse

The following sounds occur only in Perso-Arabic loanwords:

फ़

fa "f" sound as in **f**ake

ज़

za "z" sound as in **z**ebra

क़

qa same as the "k" sound in s**k**irt but said in the back of the throat. You almost should hear a deep, scratching sound as you say this.

ख़

qh same as the kh sound in **c**opy but said in the back of the throat

ग़

qga same as the "g" sound in son**g** but said in the back of the throat

Now let's combine the full form of the vowels that we have learned with a consonant. In combination with consonants, vowels are often written in short-form symbols known as *mātrā*.

Here is a chart showing common vowels in combination with the sound *ka*:

क
ka

का
ka + ā

कि
ka + i

की
ka + ī

कु
ka + u

कू
ka + ū

के
ka + e

कै
ka + ai

को
ka + o

कौ
ka + au

In Hindi it is common for some words to end in a nasalized vowel. In this book, *N* will be used in words to indicate nasalization. In *Devanāgarī*, a *chandra bindu* (ँ) is used above the top line. This *chandra bindu* symbol can also be written as a single *bindu* (ं) when there is a vowel character that extends above the line. Please note that in the current use of Hindi, the single *bindu* is often used for both single and *chandra bindu*.

<u>EXAMPLE</u>:

The word "yes" in Hindi is हाँ and, using *N* for nasalization, will be written in this book as (*hāN*). Again, the *N* is used merely to indicate that the word should be pronounced with a nasalized sound and should not be pronounced as a hard "n." Also note that in the Hindi-English romanized dictionary section, all diacritics have been ignored in order to alphabetize the words according to the English dictionary. Therefore, for the purposes of this book, *N* is considered to be a diacritic and has been ignored in ordering the dictionary.

Conjunct Consonants

As words are written, many consonants take on a shortened form. When consonants are combined in this way, the pronunciation becomes shorter. Some form characters that look quite different when combined. For example, the Hindi word for "what" is *kyā* and is composed of the letters *ka, ya* and the vowel *ā*. The *ka* and *ya* sounds are combined to make *kya*. This way, the word is pronounced *kyā* and not *kayā:*

ka + ya = kya	क + य = क्य

In addition to the above example, here are some important ones to note:

pa + ya = pya	प + य = प्य
va + ra = vra	व + र = व्र
ga + ya = gya	ग + य = ग्य
ca + cha = ccha	च + छ = च्छ
ca + ca = cca	च + च = च्च
ṭa + ṭha = ṭṭha	ट + ठ = ट्ठ
ṭa + ra = ṭra	ट + र = ट्र
ta + ta = tta	त + त = त्त
da + dha = ddha	द + ध = द्ध
da + ra = dra	द + र = द्र
dha + ya = dhya	ध + य = ध्य

pa + ra = pra	प + र = प्र
ta + ra = tra	त + र = त्र
ḍa + ra = ḍra	ड + र = ड्र
ka + ra = kra	क + र = क्र
ka + ṣa = kṣa	क + ष = क्ष
ga + ya = gya	ग + य = ज्ञ

Please note that when the र (*ra*) sound falls in shortened form before a consonant, it is written above the line as a "flying r" as shown here:

मार्ग
mārg

Note that the "flying r" is taking the place of the र letter here.

When the र falls after a consonant, it is usually written in short form as a ्र angling out to the left of the consonant character, or as a ^ below the letter. As in the case of conjunct consonants discussed previously, the combination of these two sounds will shorten the duration of pronunciation:

da + ra = dr	द + र = द्र
ṭ + ra = ṭr	ट + र = ट्र

A Brief Hindi Grammar

The purpose of this chapter is to provide a very basic grammar of Hindi, covering the most common elements to enable the traveler to expand beyond the phrasebook and begin to form his or her own sentences. Hindi is very flexible in its sentence structure. In general, the language follows the SUBJECT - OBJECT - VERB format. Articles as English speakers know them are not used in Hindi. However, sometimes the word *ek* ("one") is used to denote "a" as in "a book" or "a boy." At times you also will be saying *voh* (he, she, it, that) when you would normally use "the" or "that" for distant objects, and *yeh* (he, she it, this) in cases when you normally would use "the" or "this" for nearby objects in English.

Nouns

In Hindi there are masculine (*m.*) and feminine (*f.*) nouns. There are two types of masculine nouns:

Type I ends in *ā* in the singular and *e* in the plural:

SINGULAR	PLURAL
boy	boys
लड़का	लड़के
laṛkā	*laṛke*

Type II masculine nouns have irregular endings and their gender is not always obvious. In the plural, they do not change their endings:

SINGULAR	PLURAL
man	men
आदमी	आदमी
ādmī	*ādmī*

In addition, nouns that come directly from Sanskrit such as *rājā* (king) remain the same in both singular and plural forms. There is no way to recognize these at first. You will learn them by reading.

There are also two types of feminine nouns in Hindi. Type I feminine nouns end in *ī* in the singular and *iyāN* in the plural (remember that the *N* is not to be pronounced; it merely denotes nasalization).

candy	candies
मिठाई	मिठाइयाँ
miṭhāī	*miṭhāiyāN*

Type II feminine nouns, like Type II masculine nouns, also have irregular endings. However, Type II feminine nouns end in the nasalized *eN* sound in the plural.

book	books
किताब	किताबें
kitāb	*kitābeN*

Personal & Demonstrative Pronouns

The following is a chart of personal pronouns used in Hindi. Note that unlike in English, there are three different ways to say "you" in Hindi. The pronoun *tū* is used in the least formal or most personal situations such as when addressing young children or animals and also in intimate situations when a devotee addresses his or her God. *Tum* is used among friends and contemporaries. *Āp* is the more formal and respectful way to address someone and always should be used while traveling around India. *Āp* also should always be used with elders, teachers, etc. Note that it is not always necessary to use personal pronouns in Hindi because the verbs are conjugated according to person. For example, *maiN jātā hūN*, or "I go," means the same thing if you drop the personal pronoun *maiN* and just say *jātā hūN*. Pronouns definitely will be used in cases of address or emphasis.

मैं
maiN I

तू
tū you (*s.int.*)

यह
yah or *yeh* he/she/it (*s.*) (also used for people or objects near to the

speaker). This is usually pronounced as *yeh* and will be transcribed this way for the purposes of this book.

वह
voh — he/she/it (*s.*) (also used for people or objects at a distance from the speaker). Again, this normally would be transcribed as *vah* based on the *Devanāgarī*, but the most common pronunciation is *voh*.

तुम
tum — you (*s.fam. & pl.fam.*)

आप
āp — you (*s.for. & pl.for./respectful*)

हम
ham — we

ये
ye — these/they (he/she/it (*pl.*))

वे
ve — those/they (he/she/it (*pl.*))

Postpositions & Nouns

Postpositions follow nouns and personal pronouns. In Hindi, when a plural noun is followed by a postposition the noun changes into a form known as the oblique. Here are some examples of postpositions in Hindi and how they alter the noun in a sentence:

को	पर	के साथ
ko	*par*	*ke sāth*
to	at/on	with/along with

लड़का + के साथ	=	लड़के के साथ
laṛkā + ke sāth	=	*laṛke ke sāth*
boy + with	=	with the boy
लड़के + के साथ	=	लड़कों के साथ
laṛke + ke sāth	=	*laṛkoN ke sāth*
boys + with	=	with the boys (oblique form)
लड़की + के साथ	=	लड़की के साथ
laṛkī + ke sāth	=	*laṛkī ke sāth*
girl + with	=	with the girl (no change)
लड़कियाँ + के साथ	=	लड़कियों के साथ
laṛkiyāN + ke sāth	=	*laṛkiyoN ke sāth*
girls + with	=	with the girls (oblique form)

Possessive

You can make regular nouns possessive by inserting the particles *kā* (m.s.), *kī* (f.s.), *ke* (m.pl.), or *kī* (f.pl.) in between the noun and the object. These words are best translated as "of" and agree with the object in gender and number. "Bill's house" thus can be thought of as "house of Bill."

Here are some more examples:

बिल का नाम
Bil kā nām "name of Bill" or "Bill's name"
(*lit*. "Bill of name")

बिल की किताब
Bil kī kitāb "book of Bill" or "Bill's book"
(*lit*. "Bill of book")

बिल की किताबें
Bil kī kitābeN "books of Bill" or "Bill's books"
(*lit*. "Bill of books")

बिल के लड़के
Bil ke laṛke "boys of Bill" or "Bill's boys"
(*lit*. "Bill of boys")

Please note there are certain situations in which, out of respect, you should use the plural form.

For example, *us kā pitā jī* means "his father," but out of respect for someone's father, you should replace the *kā* with *ke*, the *m.pl.* form. This is similar to the use of the personal pronoun *āp* that is used for the *s.* and *pl.* and shows respect.

Possessive Pronouns

Pronouns in the possessive will agree with the object in gender and number. Note: the pronouns *yeh* (it, he, she, this), *voh* (it, he, she, that), *ye* (these), and *ve* (those) have alternate possessive forms as shown below. In the possessive form or when followed by any postposition, they change into *is, us, in,* and *un* respectively. This will become clearer in the phrasebook chapters.

MASCULINE *s./pl.*	MEANING	FEMININE *s./pl.*
मेरा / मेरे *merā / mere*	my	मेरी / मेरी *merī / merī*
तेरा / तेरे *terā / tere*	your	तेरी / तेरी *terī / terī*
इस का / इस के *is kā / is ke*	his/her/its *(nearby)*	इस की / इस की *is kī / is kī*

MASCULINE *s./pl.*	MEANING	FEMININE *s./pl.*
उस का / उस के *us kā / us ke*	his/her/its *(at a distance)*	उस की / उस की *us kī / us kī*
तुम्हारा / तुम्हारे *tumhārā / tumhāre*	your (*fam.*)	तुम्हारी / तुम्हारी *tumhārī / tumhārī*
आप का / आप के *āp kā / āp ke*	your (*for.*)	आप की / आप की *āp kī / āp kī*
हमारा / हमारे *hamārā / hamāre*	our	हमारी / हमारी *hamārī / hamārī*
इन का / इन के *in kā / in ke*	their/these *(nearby)*	इन की / इन की *in kī / in kī*
उन का / उन के *un kā / un ke*	their/those (*at a distance*)	उन की / उन की *un kī / un kī*

EXAMPLE:

ghar means "house" in Hindi and is a noun *(m.s.)*. Using the chart above, "my house" would be *merā ghar*. Likewise, *kitāb* means "book" and is a noun (*f.s.)*. "Our book" would be *hamārī kitāb*.

Adjectives

Now that we have learned the use of *kā, kī,* and *ke* we easily can explore the use of adjectives in Hindi. Type I adjectives also agree with the noun in gender and number. Let's use the common word *acchā,* which means "good" or "nice." In some situations, *acchā* also can mean "okay" when responding to someone repeatedly in a conversation to show your understanding of what he or she is saying (like the use of "uh-huh" in U.S. English).

अच्छा खाना

acchā khānā good food (implies "tasty food" just as in English)

अच्छी जानकारी

acchī jānkārī good information

अच्छे लड़के

acche laṛke good boys

अच्छी किताबें

acchī kitābeN good books

Other examples of Type I adjectives are *choṭā,* which means "little" or "small" and *baṛā,* which means "big." Endings will inflect just as in the above example with *acchā.*

Type II adjectives do not end in a vowel and generally do not change their endings to make agreement. For example, *lāl* means "red" and does not change at all.

Verbs

This section will discuss commonly used verb forms. For each form, the conjugations will be shown both in romanized Hindi and in the *Devanāgarī* script so that you can begin to recognize the "shape" of the language. Hindi verbs in "dictionary" or "infinitive" forms are composed of a verb stem and the suffix *nā*. For example, *khānā* means "to eat" and is composed of the stem *khā* and the common verb ending *nā*. Most verbs are conjugated by dropping the *nā* suffix and attaching various endings to the stem.

Let's start by conjugating the verb *honā*, which means "to be" or "to exist."

मैं हूँ
maiN hūN
I am

तुम हो
tum ho
you (*s.fam. & pl.fam.*) are

तू है
tū hai
you (*s.int.*) are

आप हैं
āp haiN
you (*s.for. & pl.for.*) are

	हम हैं *ham haiN* we are
यह है *yeh hai* he/she/it/this is	ये हैं *ye haiN* these/they (*s.for. & pl.for.*) are
वह ह *voh hai* he/she/it/that is	वे हैं *ve haiN* those/they (*s.for. & pl.for.*) are

Imperfect past of *honā*

At this point the simple imperfect past forms of *honā* will be introduced, as they will be used in other verb conjugations. Note that while there is no gender distinction in present tense forms of *honā*, a slight difference does exist in the simple past forms for all persons. We will keep it simple by displaying the past forms like this:

MASCULINE		FEMININE	
singular:		singular:	
था	*thā*	थी	*thī*
plural:		plural:	
थे	*the*	थीं	*thīN*

Example, present tense:

मैं नई दिल्ली में हूँ।
maiN naī dillī meN hūN.
I am in New Delhi.
(*lit.* "I New Delhi in am")

Example, past tense:

मैं नई दिल्ली में था।
maiN naī dillī meN thā.
I was in New Delhi.
(*lit.* "I New Delhi in was")

To illustrate the habitual, progressive, past, future, and imperative forms of Hindi verbs, the verb *jānā* "to go" will be used in each example.

Habitual Present (or Imperfect Present)

The habitual form of the Hindi verb indicates activities or actions that routinely take place. For instance, "I go to school" indicates that the action of going to school takes place perhaps daily, and certainly has happened more than once. This form uses the conjugated verb *honā* as a type of auxiliary verb. Note that in this case it is not a traditional auxiliary verb since more than just the verb stem of *jānā* is being used. Both are conjugated according to gender and number.

MASCULINE:	FEMININE:
मैं जाता हूँ *maiN jātā hūN* I go	मैं जाती हूँ *maiN jātī hūN* I go
तू जाता है *tū jātā hai* you (*s.int.*) go	तू जाती है *tū jātī hai* you (*s.int.*) go
यह जाता है *yeh jātā hai* he/it/this goes	यह जाती है *yeh jātī hai* she/it/this goes
वह जाता है *voh jātā hai* he/it/that goes	वह जाती है *voh jātī hai* she/it/that goes
तुम जाते हो *tum jāte ho* you (*s.fam. & pl.fam.*) go	तुम जाती हो *tum jātī ho* you (*s.fam. & pl.fam.*) go
आप जाते हैं *āp jāte haiN* you (*s.for. & pl.for.*) go	आप जाती हैं *āp jātī haiN* you (*s.for. & pl.for.*) go
हम जाते हैं *ham jāte haiN* we go	हम जाती हैं *ham jātī haiN* we go
ये जाते हैं *ye jāte haiN* these/they go	ये जाती हैं *ye jātī haiN* these/they go

वे जाते हैं	वे जाती हैं
ve jāte haiN	*ve jātī haiN*
those/they go	those/they go

To put the above forms in the past tense, you can use the same past endings as in the case of *honā*:

MASCULINE		FEMININE	
singular:		singular:	
था	*thā*	*थी*	*thī*
plural:		plural:	
थे	*the*	*थीं*	*thīN*

However, please note that you are forming the "habitual" past, so the phrases must be translated as "I used to go," "we used to go," and "they used to go." In English one might say "I used to go to that restaurant when I lived in New York," implying that one "went to the restaurant" habitually, or more than once.

EXAMPLE:

आप जाते हैं
āp jāte haiN
you (*pl.for.*) go

We simply take the masculine, plural past ending of थे *(the)* and substitute it for the present tense conjugation हैं (*haiN*) that is shown above:

आप जाते थे
āp jāte the
you (*pl.for.*) used to go

Progressive

The progressive form of the Hindi verb is closely translated as the "-ing" form of the English verb. It indicates present action. The "-ing" form of the Hindi verb is formed by using the verb stem, in this case *jā*, and removing the *nā* stem to add an alternate ending:

MASCULINE:	FEMININE:
मैं जा रहा हूँ *maiN jā rahā hūN* I am going	मैं जा रही हूँ *maiN jā rahī hūN* I am going
तू जा रहा है *tū jā rahā hai* you (*s.int.*) are going	तू जा रही है *tū jā rahī hai* you (*s.int.*) are going
यह जा रहा है *yeh jā rahā hai* he/it/this is going	यह जा रही है *yeh jā rahī hai* she/it/this is going
वह जा रहा है *voh jā rahā hai* he/it/that is going	वह जा रही है *voh jā rahī hai* she/it/that is going

तुम जा रहे हो *tum jā rahe ho* you (*s.fam. & pl.fam.*) are going	तुम जा रही हो *tum jā rahī ho* you (*s.fam. & pl.fam.*) are going
आप जा रहे हैं *āp jā rahe haiN* you (*s.for. & pl.for.*) are going	आप जा रही हैं *āp jā rahī haiN* you (*s.for. & pl.for.*) are going
हम जा रहे हैं *ham jā rahe haiN* we are going	हम जा रही हैं *ham jā rahī haiN* we are going
ये जा रहे हैं *ye jā rahe haiN* these/they are going	ये जा रही हैं *ye jā rahī haiN* these/they are going
वे जा रहे हैं *ve jā rahe haiN* those/they are going	वे जा रही हैं *ve jā rahī haiN* those/they are going

Past Perfect

Most verbs form the past perfect tense by retaining their original stems and adding *ā, ī, e,* or *īN* endings. When the verb stem ends in a vowel, such as *khānā* ("to eat"), a *yā* is inserted.

In the past perfect tense in Hindi, some verbs take a *ne* particle after the subject. In most cases, transitive verbs will take a *ne* if an object follows immediately after the verb. Most intransitive verbs do not take a *ne* because there is usually no direct object. When a verb requires *ne*, the personal pronoun used will take the same form as it does when followed by any other postposition. Remember that *yeh* becomes *is*, *voh* becomes *us*, etc. as illustrated in the pronouns section.

मैंने सेब खाया
maiN ***ne*** *seb khāyā*
I ate an apple

Note that in this example above, the past perfect tense of the verb is in agreement in gender and number with the *object*, not the *subject*. This is because *khānā*, "to eat," is a transitive verb and will take the *ne* marker. Transitive verbs in the past perfect usually refer to events that have happened with a definite end. For example, "I ate an apple" is an event that has happened already. In other cases with intransitive verbs, such as "I went to New York," the verb agrees with the subject, I, not the object, New York:

मैं न्यू योर्क गया *m.* / गई *f.*
maiN nyū york gayā m. / *gaī* f.
I went to New York

When there is a mixed group of men and women, the masculine form generally is used. This *ne* verb element can be quite confusing in the beginning. Right now it is enough to be aware of it so that you can pay attention to that form as it appears in the different phrasebook chapters.

Some verbs in the past perfect tense are irregular because their stems change. Such verbs include *karnā,* "to do," where the *kar* stem changes to *ki*; *denā,* "to give," where the *de* stem changes to *di*; and *lenā,* "to take," where the *le* stem changes to *li*. The past perfect conjugation of the verb *jānā* is also irregular as the stem of the verb changes to *ga*:

MASCULINE:	FEMININE:
मैं गया *maiN gayā* I went	मैं गई *maiN gaī* I went
तू गया *tū gayā* you (*s.int.*) went	तू गई *tū gaī* you (*s.int.*) went
यह गया *yeh gayā* he/it/this went	यह गई *yeh gaī* she/it/this went

वह गया *voh gayā* he/it/that went	वह गई *voh gaī* she/it/that went
तुम गये *tum gaye* you (*s.fam. &* *pl.fam.*) went	तुम गईं *tum gaīN* you (*s.fam. &* *pl.fam.*) went
आप गये *āp gaye* you (*s.for. &* *pl.for.*) went	आप गईं *āp gaīN* you (*s.for. &* *pl.for.*) went
हम गये *ham gaye* we went	हम गईं *ham gaīN* we went
ये गये *ye gaye* these/they went	ये गईं *ye gaīN* these/they went
वे गये *ve gaye* those/they went	वे गईं *ve gaīN* those/they went

While *jānā* is irregular in its past perfect tense, you still can learn how to conjugate other verbs by paying attention to the vowel endings for each form. Most masculine singular endings are *ā*, feminine singular *ī*, masculine plural *e*, and feminine plural *īN*. For a regular verb such as *bolnā*, you would merely attach the aforementioned endings to the verb stem *bol* to form the perfected past. For verb stems that end in a vowel such as *khānā*, you would add *yā* to the verb stem *khā* for masculine singular, *yī* for feminine singular, *ye* for masculine plural, and *yīN* for feminine plural.

Of course, beyond *jānā* there are many more irregular verbs in Hindi. The verb *honā* also has completely unique forms in the past perfective. In this basic Hindi grammar it is not possible to include the conjugation for all of the irregular verbs. However, when you work with the dictionary and phrasebook chapters you will begin to see a pattern and will be able to figure out many of these conjugations on your own.

Future

In the future tense, *jānā* retains its original stem. Verb stems that end in *ū* or *ī* shorten their stems to *u* and *i* before adding the future endings. For example, *chūṭnā* means "to be released." In this case the long *ū* stem in *chū* would be shortened to *chu* before conjugating it in future tense.

Future form of *jānā*:

MASCULINE:	FEMININE:
मैं जाऊँगा *maiN jāūNgā* I will go	मैं जाऊँगी *maiN jāūNgī* I will go
तू जायेगा *tū jāyegā* you (*s.int.*) will go	तू जायेगी *tū jāyegī* you (*s.int.*) will go
यह जायेगा *yeh jāyegā* he/it/this will go	यह जायेगी *yeh jāyegī* she/it/this will go
वह जायेगा *voh jāyegā* he/it/that will go	वह जायेगी *voh jāyegī* she/it/that will go
तुम जाओगे *tum jāoge* you (*s.fam. &* *pl.fam.*) will go	तुम जाओगी *tum jāogī* you (*s.fam. &* *pl.fam.*) will go
आप जायेंगे *āp jāyeNge* you (*s.for. &* *pl.for.*) will go	आप जायेंगी *āp jāyeNgī* you (*s.for. &* *pl.for.*) will go
हम जायेंगे *ham jāyeNge* we will go	हम जायेंगी *ham jāyeNgī* we will go

ये जायेंगे *ye jāyeNge* these/they will go	ये जायेंगीं *ye jāyeNgī* these/they will go
वे जायेंगे *ve jāyeNge* those/they will go	वे जायेंगी *ve jāyeNgī* those/they will go

Imperative/Command

To form an imperative using the personal pronoun *āp*, simply add the *-iye* ending to the verb stem:

जाइये
jāiye
please go

To form an imperative of a verb when addressing someone with *tum*, simply add *-āo* to the verb stem:

जाओ
jāo
go

Commands also can be formed using the full form of the verb. This usually is most appropriate if you are addressing someone with *tum*.

EXAMPLE:

जल्दी आना
jaldī ānā
come back soon!
(*lit.* "soon to come")

Subjunctive

If you want to say "let's go" or "shall we get going?" in Hindi, you will need to use the subjunctive form. The subjunctive form will not be discussed in great detail here, but it is formed by taking the future ending off of the verb and leaving what remains. The subjunctive can be used to express possibility such as "shall we get going?" as well as wishes or desires such as "may God bless you" or "may you be filled with peace and happiness."

EXAMPLE:

हम चलें ।
ham caleN?
shall we go?
(*lit.* "shall we make a move?")

In the next example, the verb *honā* is in one of its subjunctive forms of *ho*:

आप की यात्रा मंगल मय हो
āp kī yātrā mangal may ho
may you have a pleasant journey

Asking Questions and Forming Sentences in Hindi

Asking questions in Hindi is a relatively easy task. Most commonly, the word *kyā* (question marker translated as "what") is placed at the very beginning of a sentence to change a statement into a question. *Kyā* also can be used before verbs such as "to be," "to eat," and "to do," to form the questions "what is," "what to eat," and "what to do," etc. Also, one can easily transform a statement in Hindi into a question, merely by raising the intonation of one's voice and omitting the question word. For example, *kyā āp bhārat gaye* "did you go to India?" has the question word *kyā* in place. However, if you drop the *kyā* in spoken Hindi and just say *āp bhārat gaye?*, the phrase has the same meaning. In traditional written Hindi, question words such as *kyā* become more important to determine context, as question marks (?) are not part of *Devanāgarī*. However, question marks are used quite often in current written Hindi.

Here are some examples of how to form questions in Hindi:

यह क्या है ।
yeh kyā hai?
What is this?
(*lit*. "this what is")

क्या यह किताब है ।
kyā yeh kitāb hai?
Is this a book?
(*lit.* "what this book is")

आप का नाम क्या है ।
āp kā nām kyā hai?
What is your name?
(*lit.* "your name what is")

The example above can be compared with the following statement:

आप का नाम ऊषा जी है ।
āp kā nām ūśā jī hai.
Your name is Usha ji.
(*lit.* "your name Usha ji is")

Now let's change the above statement into a question by placing a *kyā* at the very beginning:

क्या आप का नाम ऊषा जी है ।
kyā āp kā nām ūśā jī hai?
Is your name Usha ji?
(*lit.* "what your name Usha ji is")

Cultural note: The suffix *jī* is added to both male and female given names for politeness and should be used whenever you address a Hindi speaker, unless he or she tells you that you should not be so formal. When someone says this to you, people mean to say that they appreciate the language that you are using with them but now it is time to become more relaxed and informal. They might even ask that you start using the personal pronoun *tum* with them instead of the more formal *āp*. As a reminder, you should never use the informal and intimate pronoun *tū* at this stage.

Other common question words in Hindi include:

कब
kab
when

कैसा
kaisā
how

कितना
kitnā
how much/many

कहाँ
kahāN
where

क्यों
kyoN
why

Here is another example with the word *kab* meaning "when." Note how flexible the word order is in Hindi, as both sentences have exactly the same meaning:

कब आप वाराणसी जा रहे हैं ।
kab āp vārāṇasī jā rahe haiN?
When are you going to Varanasi?
(*lit.* "when you Varanasi going")

आप वाराणसी कब जा रहे हैं ।
āp vārāṇasī kab jā rahe haiN?
When are you going to Varanasi?
(*lit.* "You Varanasi when going")

Expressing Comparison

One can use the particle *se* to express comparison. *Se* means "from" or "compared with." The formula is "noun-*se*-noun-adjective." Here is an example:

पैसे से प्यार अच्छा है ।
paise se, pyār acchā hai.
Love is better than money.
(*lit.* "money compared love good is")

Expressing Negation

In Hindi, the word for "no" is *nahīN*. By placing *nahīN* before any verb, you negate the meaning. *nahīN* can be used to negate almost all verb forms, except for the imperative. When addressing someone with *tum* and using an imperative, *mat* is used to negate the command. *Mat* also can be used with the *āp* form of the verb, but is less commonly used. The particle *na* also can be used in place of *mat* and is used commonly with the pronoun *āp*. Here are examples of both:

मैं नहीं जाऊँगा ।
maiN nahīN jāūNgā.
I will not go.
(*lit.* "I no will go")
(remove the *nahīN* and this sentence means "I will go.")

मैं केले नहीं खाता हूँ ।
maiN kele nahīN khātā (m.) *hūN.*
I do not eat bananas.
(remove the *nahīN* and this sentence means "I eat bananas.")

मत जाओ ।
mat jāo!
Don't go!
(remove the *mat* and this sentence means "Go!")

न जाइये ।
na jāiye.
Don't go (more polite).
(remove the *na* and this sentence means "Please go.")

na also can be used with the full form of verbs. As mentioned previously in the section on imperatives and commands, *jaldī ānā* means "come back soon." Likewise, *jaldī na ānā* would mean "don't come back anytime soon."

Expressing Wants & Needs

Wants and needs can easily be expressed with the verb *cāhanā*. *Cāhanā* can be conjugated by itself to mean "I want," "you want," etc. You also can add the full "dictionary" form of another verb to *cāhanā* in a conjugated form to say "I want to go," "do you want to eat?" etc. To conjugate the habitual present tense of *cāhanā* you can follow the same rules as illustrated previously for *jānā*. Simply replace the *jā* stem with the *cāha* stem.

EXAMPLES:

मैं सेब चाहता हूँ ।
maiN seb cāhatā (m.) *hūN*.
I want an apple.

मैं जाना चाहता हूँ ।
maiN jānā cāhatā hūN.
I want to go.
(*lit*. "I to go want")

Note that the full dictionary form of the verb "to go," *jānā*, is simply placed before the conjugation of *cāhanā*. You can insert any verb in front of *cāhanā* in this way.

Another good way to express wants and needs is with *cāhiye*. This follows the "subject-*ko*-object-*cāhiye*" formula. Some personal pronouns will take different forms when followed by the postposition *ko*. Here are some examples:

मुझको पानी चाहिये ।
mujhko pānī cāhiye.
I want/need water.

क्या उसको रात का खाना चाहिये ।
kyā usko rāt kā khānā cāhiye?
Does he/she want/need dinner?

Note on Dictionary Entries

Entries in the Hindi-English dictionary are given in romanized Hindi and alphabetized according to English dictionary order to aid the beginner. Diacritical markings do not affect the order of entries. The letter *N* indicates a nasalized sound and is considered a diacritical marking, so it also has not been taken into account in the alphabetical order.

Hindi-English Dictionary

A

ab अब *adv.* now
abhāvanīy अभावनीय *adj.* inconceivable
abhī-abhī अभी-अभी *adv.* right now
abhimānī अभिमानी *adj.* conceited
abhinetā अभिनेता *n.m.* actor
abhī tak अभी तक *adv.* already
acānak अचानक *adj.* suddenly
acchā अच्छा *adj.* good, nice
adālat अदालत *n.f.* court (legal)
ādar आदर *n.m.* respect
ādat आदत *n.f.* habit
ādhā आधा *n.m.* half
ādhāsīsī आधासीसी *n.f.* migraine
aNdherā अँधेरा *adj. & n.m.* dark; darkness
adhyāpak अध्यापक *n.m.* teacher
ādmī आदमी *n.m.* man
āg आग *n.f.* fire
āge आगे *adv.* ahead
aglā अगला *adj.* next
āgman आगमन *n.m.* arrival
aNgrezī अंग्रेज़ी *n.f.* English
aNgūṭhī अँगूठी *n.f.* ring
āiskrīm आइसक्रीम *n.f.* ice cream
aisparin ऐस्पिरिन *n.f.* aspirin
aiśvary ऐश्वर्य *n.m.* luxury
aitihāsik ऐतिहासिक *adj.* historical

āj आज *adv. & n.m.* today
ajīb अजीब *adj.* strange
ajnabī अजनबी *n.m.* stranger
āj rāt आज रात *adv. & n.m.* tonight
ākār आकार *n.m.* shape
ākāś आकाश *n.m.* sky
akelā अकेला *adj.* alone
āNkh आँख *n.f.* eye
aksar अक्सर *adv.* often
āksījan आकसीजन *n.m.* oxygen
alag अलग *adj.* different, separate
alārm gharī अलार्म घड़ी *n.f.* alarm clock
allāh अल्लाह *n.m.* God (Islam)
ālsī आलसी *adj.* lazy
ām आम *adj.* typical (common)
amīr अमीर *adj.* wealthy
ānā आना *v.i.* come (to)
ānand आनंद *n.m.* bliss
anannās अनन्नास *n.m.* pineapple
aṇḍā अण्डा *n.m.* egg
andar अन्दर *adv.* inside
andar ke kapṛe अन्दर के कपड़े *n.m.* underwear
andhā अंधा *adj.* blind
āndolit karnā अंदोलित करना *v.t.* disturb (to agitate)
angulī अंगुली *n.f.* finger
angūr अंगूर *n.m.* grape
angūr kā bāqg अंगूर का बाग़ *n.m.* vineyard
angūṭhā अंगूठा *n.m.* thumb
aniścit अनिश्चित *adj.* uncertain (doubtful)
anjān अनजान *adj.* unknown

anokhā अनोखा *adj.* odd (strange)
ant अंत *n.m.* end
antariks अन्तरिक्ष *n.m.* space (outer)
antārkṣī अंतारक्षी *adj.* cosmic
antarrāṣṭrīy अंतरराष्ट्रीय *adj.* international
āntim अन्तिम *adj.* last (final)
anubandh अनुबंध *n.m.* contract
anumati अनुमति *n.f.* permission
anumati denā अनुमति देना *v.i. & v.t.* allow (to), permit (to)
anumati-patr अनुमति-पत्र *n.m.* permit
anuvād अनुवाद *n.m.* translation
anuvād karnā अनुवाद करना *v.t.* translate (to)
āp आप *pron.for.m.f.* you
apmānjanak अपमानजनक *adj.* offensive (insulting)
aprādhī अपराधी *n.m.* criminal
aprāpti अप्राप्ति *n.f.* loss
āpravās आप्रवास *n.m.* immigration
āpravāsī आप्रवासी *adj. & n.m.* immigrant
āpreśn आप्रेशन *n.m.* operation
āp svayam आप स्वयं *pron.for.m.f.* yourself
ārām आराम *n.m.* relaxation, rest
ārāmdāyak आरामदायक *adj.* comfortable
ārḍr karnā ऑर्डर करना *v.t.* order (to place an order)
ārkṣaṇ आरक्षण *n.m.* reservation
ārkṣit karnā आरक्षित करना *v.t.* reserve (to reserve a room, seat, etc.)
arth अर्थ *n.m.* meaning
arthpūrṇ अर्थपूर्ण *adj.* meaningful

arthvyavasthā अर्थव्यवस्था *n.f.* economy
āśā आशा *n.f.* hope
asādhāraṇ असाधारण *adj.* unusual
asal meN असल में *adv.* actually
asamāntā असमानता *n.f.* inequality
asambhav असंभव *adj.* impossible
āsān आसान *adj.* easy
aśānti अशान्ति *n.f.* disturbance
āścarya आश्चर्य *n.m.* surprise
aścaryajanak आश्चर्यजनक *adj.* amazing
āśīrvād आशीर्वाद *n.m.* blessing
aslī असली *adj.* real
aspatāl अस्पताल *n.m.* hospital
aspatāl gāṛī अस्पताल गाड़ी *n.f.* ambulance
asthāyī अस्थायी *adj.* temporary
aśuddh अशुद्ध *adj.* improper (wrong)
asurikshit असुरक्षित *adj.* unsafe
asuvidhā असुविधा *n.f.* disadvantage
āṭā आटा *n.m.* flour
aNtaṛī अँतड़ी *n.f.* intestines
atithi अतिथि *n.m.f.* guest
ātmā आत्मा *n.m.* spirit (soul)
ātmhatyā आत्महत्या *n.f.* suicide
ātmik आत्मिक *adj.* spiritual
aur और *conj.* and
aurat औरत *n.f.* lady (woman)
auratoN kā ḍākṭar औरतों का डॉकटर *n.m.* gynecologist (male, *lit.* "women's doctor")
auratoN kī ḍākṭar औरतों की डॉकटर *n.f.* gynecologist (female, *lit.* "women's doctor")
āvaśyak आवश्यक *adj.* necessary

āvāz आवाज़ *n.f.* voice
aviśvāsnīy अविश्वासनीय *adj.* unbelievable
avivāhit अविवाहित *adj.* unmarried
avsar अवसर *n.m.* opportunity

B

bacāo! बचाओ *interj.* help!
baccā बच्चा *n.m.* child
bacce बच्चे *n.m.* children
bacce ko dekhne vālā *m.* / **vālī** *f.* बच्चे को देखने वाला *n.m.* / वाली *n.f.* babysitter
baccī बच्ची *n.f.* child
bachaṛā *m.* / **bachaṛī** *f.* बछड़ा *n.m.* / बछड़ी *n.f.* calf
bādal बादल *n.m.* cloud
badalnā बदलना *v.i. & v.t.* change (to)
badbū बदबू *n.f.* smell (bad odor)
badhāī ho! बधाई हो *interj.* congratulations!
badhazamī बदहज़मी *n.f.* indigestion
badlā बदला *n.m.* revenge
bād meN बाद में *adv.* after (later)
bahādur बहादुर *adj.* brave
bāhar बाहर *n.m.* outside
baharā बहरा *adj.* deaf
bahas karnā बहस करना *v.i. & v.t.* argue (to)
bahumat बहुमत *n.m.* majority
bahut बहुत *adj.* many (a lot); very
baiNgan बैंगन *n.m.* eggplant
baiNganī बैंगनी *adj.* purple
baiNk बैंक *n.f.* bank
bairā बैरा *n.m.* waiter

baiṭhanā बैठना *v.i.* sit (to)
baiṭrī बैटरी *n.f.* battery
bakarā बकरा *n.m.* goat
bākī बाकी *n.f.* rest (remainder)
baksā बक्सा *n.m.* box
bal बल *n.m.* strength (bodily)
bāl बाल *n.m.* hair (of head)
balātkār बलात्कार *n.m.* rape
balī बली *adj.* strong
bāliyāN बालियाँ *n.f.* earrings
bāl kaṭāī बाल कटाई *n.m.* haircut
bāloN kā braś बालों का ब्रश *n.m.* hairbrush
bālṭī बाल्टी *n.f.* bucket
bālū बालू *n.m.* sand
banānā बनाना *v.t.* make (to)
band gāṛī बंद गाड़ी *n.f.* van
bandī बन्दी *n.m.* prisoner
band karnā बन्द करना *v.t.* close (to)
bandūk बन्दूक *n.f.* gun
bāqg बाग़ *n.m.* garden
baqhśīś बख़शशि *n.m.* tip (gratuity usually given in advance)
bār बार *n.f.* bar (café)
bāṛ बाड़ *n.m.* fence
baṛā बड़ा *adj.* big, large
barābarī बराबरी *n.f.* equality
barf बर्फ़ *n.f.* ice
baṛhiyā बढ़िया *adj.* excellent
bāriś बारिश *n.f.* rain
bas! बस *interj.* enough! (stop!)
bas बस *n.m.* bus

bassṭāp बसस्टाप *n.f.* bus station
batānā बताना *v.t.* tell (to)
bātcīt बातचीत *n.f.* conversation
bātcīt karnā बातचीत करना *v.t.* talk (to)
bāNṭ denā बाँट देना *v.t.* share (to)
battī बत्ती *n.f.* lightbulb
bauddhda बौद्ध *adj. & n.m.f.* Buddhist
bāyāN बायाँ *adj.* left
bāzār बाज़ार *n.m.* market
beārām बेआराम *adj.* uncomfortable
bebī fūd बेबी फूड *n.f.* baby food
becain बेचैन *adj.* impatient
becnā बेचना *v.t.* sell (to)
beghar बेघर *adj.* homeless
behn बहन *n.f.* sister
behoś बेहोश *adj.* unconscious
behoś ho jānā बेहोश हो जाना *v.i.* faint (to)
behośī बेहोशी *n.f.* unconsciousness
beīmān बेईमान *adj.* dishonest
bekār बेकार *adj.* useless
bel बेल *n.m.* vine
berozgārī बेरोज़गारी *n.f.* unemployment
beṭā बेटा *n.m.* son
beṭī बेटी *n.f.* daughter
bhāg भाग *n.m.* part
bhāNg भाँग *n.f.* hashish
bhāg jānā भाग जाना *v.i.* run away (to)
bhāgya भाग्य *n.m.* luck
bhāī भाई *n.m.* brother
bhangur भंगुर *adj.* fragile
bhārī भारी *adj.* heavy

bhāṣā भाषा *n.f.* language
bhāṣṇ भाषण *n.m.* speech (formal)
bhāt भात *n.m.* rice (cooked)
bhavan भवन *n.m.* building
bhaviṣya भविष्य *n.m.* future
bhed-bhāv भेद-भाव *n.m.* discrimination
bhejnā भेजना *v.t.* send (to)
bheṛ भेड़ *n.f.* sheep
bheṛiyā भेड़िया *n.m.* wolf
bhī भी *adv.* too (also)
bhikhārī भिखारी *n.f.* beggar
bhīṛ भीड़ *n.f.* crowd
bhojan भोजन *n.m.* meal
bholā-bhālā भोला-भाला *adj.* naive
bhraṣṭācār भ्रष्टाचार *n.m.* corruption
bhugtān भुगतान *n.m.* payment
bhūkamp भूकंप *n.m.* earthquake
bhūkh भूख *n.m.* hunger
bhūkhā भूखा *adj.* hungry
bhūl भूल *n.f.* mistake
bhūl jānā भूल जाना *v.i.* forget (to)
bhūmi भूमि *n.f.* land (soil)
bhyānak भयानक *adj.* awful
bhyankar भयंकर *adj.* terrible
bīc meN बीच में *prep.* between
bijalī बिजली *n.f.* electricity; lightning
bikrī बिक्री *n.f.* sale
bilauṭā बिलैटा *n.m.* kitten
billī बिल्ली *n.f.* cat
bīmā बीमा *n.m.* insurance
bīmār बीमार *adj.* ill

bīmārī बीमारी *n.f.* illness
bistar बिस्तर *n.m.* bed
bītā huā बीता हुआ *adj.* past
biyar बियर *n.f.* beer
bolnā बोलना *v.i. & v.t.* speak (to); say (to)
bonā बोना *v.t.* plant (to)
botal बोतल *n.f.* bottle
botal kā pānī बोतल का पानी *n.m.* mineral water (*lit.* "bottled water")
botal kholne vālā बोटल खोलने वाला *n.m.* bottle opener
buddhimān बुद्धिमान *adj.* smart (intelligent)
būḍhā बूढा *adj.* old (person)
budhvār बुधवार *n.m.* Wednesday
bulānā बुलाना *v.i. & v.t.* call (to summon)
buqhār बुख़ार *n.m.* fever
burā बुरा *adj.* bad
būṭ बूट *n.m.* boots

C

cābī चाबी *n.f.* key
cādar चादर *n.f.* sheet (for bed)
cāNdī चाँदी *n.f.* silver
cāhanā चाहना *v.i. & v.t.* need (to); want (to)
cāi चाय *n.f.* tea
cakkar चक्कर *n.m.* dizziness
cakra चक्र *n.m.* wheel
cāl चाल *n.f.* speed
calānā चलाना *v.t.* drive (to drive a vehicle)
calnā चलना *v.i.* move (to)

calnā rehnā चलना रहना *v.i.* continue (to)
camelī चमेली *n.f.* jasmine
cammac चम्मच *n.m.* spoon
camṛā चमड़ा *n.m.* leather
camṛī चमड़ी *n.f.* skin (human)
canā चना *n.m.* chickpea
candan चंदन *n.m.* sandalwood
candra चन्द्र *n.m.* moon
cāqū चाकू *n.m.* knife
caṛhānā चढ़ाना *v.t.* offer (to)
caṛhāvā चढ़ावा *n.m.* offering (religious)
caśmā चश्मा *n.m.* eyeglasses
caṭāī चटाई *n.f.* mat; mattress
caṭṭān चट्टान *n.f.* rock
caṭṭānoN par caḍhnā चट्टानों पर चढना *v.t.* rock climb (to)
cauṛā चौड़ा *adj.* wide
caurāhā चौराहा *n.m.* intersection (of roads)
cāval चावल *n.m.* rice (uncooked)
cek चेक *n.m.* check
cetāvanī चेतावनी *n.f.* warning
cetāvanī denā चेतावनी देना *v.t.* warn (to)
chajjā छज्जा *n.m.* terrace (balcony)
chat छत *n.f.* roof
chātā छाता *n.m.* umbrella
chātī छाती *n.f.* chest
chāyā छाया *n.f.* shadow, shade
chilkā छिल्का *n.m.* shell (of nuts, etc.)
choṛ denā छोड़ देना *v.t.* quit (to)
choṭā छोटा *adj.* little (small), short (length & height)

chūnā छूना *v.t.* touch (to)
chuṭkārā छुटकारा *n.m.* relief (from burden)
chuṭṭī छुट्टी *n.f.* vacation (holiday)
cigreṭ pīnā सिग्रेट पीना *v.t.* smoke (to smoke cigarettes)
cilam चिलम *n.f.* pipe
cillānā चिल्लाना *v.t.* shout (to)
cīnī चीनी *adj. & n.f.* Chinese; sugar
cintā चिन्ता *n.f.* anxiety, worry
cintā karnā चिन्ता करना *v.t.* worry (to)
cintan चिन्तन *n.m.* reflection
ciṛiyā चिड़िया *n.f.* bird
ciṛiyāghar चिड़ियाघर *n.m.* zoo
cīNṭī चींटी *n.f.* ant
citrakār चित्रकार *n.m.* painter
ciṭṭhī चिट्ठी *n.f.* letter
cīz चीज़ *n.f.* thing
cor चोर *n.m.* thief
coṭ चोट *n.f.* injury; bruise
coṭī चोटी *n.f.* peak (mountain)
cuhiyā चुहिया *n.f.* mouse
cūlhā चूल्हा *n.m.* stove
cummā चुम्मा *n.m.* kiss
cūmnā चूमना *v.t.* kiss (to)
cunāv चनाव *n.m.* election
cunnā चुनना *v.t.* choose (to)
cuppī चुप्पी *n.f.* silence

D

dāb दाब *n.f.* pressure
ḍabbā डब्बा *n.m.* carton

dādā दादा *n.m.* grandfather (paternal)
dāḍhī दाढी *n.f.* beard
dādī दादी *n.f.* grandmother (paternal)
dadorā ददोरा *n.m.* rash
daftar दफ़्तर *n.m.* office
dahī दही *n.m.* yogurt
dāhinā दाहिना *adj.* right (direction)
dāh sanskār दाह संस्कार *n.m.* funeral (Hindu cremation rite)
dāī दाई *n.f.* midwife
dainik दैनिक *adj.* daily
ḍāk डाक *n.f.* mail
ḍākghar डाकघर *n.m.* post office
dakshīṇ दक्षिण *adj.* South
ḍākṭar डॉकटर *n.m.f.* doctor
ḍaliyā डलिया *n.f.* basket
dām दाम *n.m.* price
damā rogī दमा रोगी *n.m.* asthmatic
dantcikitsak दन्तचिकित्सक *n.m.* dentist
ḍar डर *n.m.* fear
dard दर्द *n.m.* pain
dard kī davā दर्द की दवा *n.f.* painkiller
dardnāk दर्दनाक *adj.* painful
darī दरी *n.f.* carpet
darjan दर्जन *n.m.* dozen (a)
ḍarnā डरना *v.i.* fear (to be afraid)
darpaṇ दर्पण *n.m.* mirror
darvāzā दरवाज़ा *n.m.* door
darzī दर्ज़ी *n.m.* tailor
das lākh दस लाख *n.m.* million (a)
dast दस्त *n.m.* diarrhea

dastakhat दस्तखत *n.m.* signature
dastāvar दस्तावर *n.m.* laxative
dāNt दाँत *n.m.* tooth
dāNt kā dard दाँत का दर्द *n.m.* toothache
daurān दैरान *prep.* during (while)
dauṛnā दौड़ना *v.i.* run (to)
davā दवा *n.f.* medicine
davāqhānā दवाख़ाना *n.m.* pharmacist
ḍāyarī डायरी *n.f.* diary
dehāt देहात *n.m.* countryside
dekhbhāl karnā देखभाल करना *v.t.* look after (to care for)
dekhnā देखना *v.t.* look (to); see (to); watch (to)
denā देना *v.t.* give (to)
der देर *adj. & n.f.* late; delay
deś देश *n.m.* country
dhāgā धागा *n.m.* string
dhakelnā धकेलना *v.t.* push (to)
dhanī धनी *adj.* rich (of money)
dhanyavād! धन्यवाद *interj.for.* thank you!
dhanyavād denā धन्यवाद देना *v.t.* thank (to)
dhārā धारा *n.f.* stream
dharm धर्म *n.m.* religion
dhārmik धार्मिक *adj.* religious
dhartī धरती *n.f.* Earth
dhātu धातु *n.f.* metal
ḍhelā ढेला *n.m.* lump
dhīraj धीरज *n.m.* patience
dhīre-dhīre धीरे-धीरे *adv.* slowly
dhobīqhānā धोबीख़ाना *n.m.* laundry
dhonā धोना *v.t.* wash (to)

ḍhonā ढोना *v.i.* carry (to)
dhūl धूल *n.f.* dirt (soil)
dhūp धूप *n.f.* sunlight
dhūp धूप *n.m.* incense
dhūp kā caśmā धूप का चश्मा *n.m.* sunglasses
dhūp se jalnā धूप से जलना *v.i.* sunburned (to become)
ḍibbā डिब्बा *n.m.* can (tin)
dikhānā दिखाना *v.t.* show (to)
dil दिल *n.m.* heart
dilcasp दिलचस्प *adj.* interesting
dimāg दिमाग *n.m.* brain
din दिन *n.m.* day
din kā khānā दिन का खाना *n.m.* lunch
diśā दिशा *n.f.* direction
dīvār दीवार *n.f.* wall
diyāsalāī दियासलाई *n.f.* match (used to light fire)
ḍiyoḍoraiNṭ डियोडोरैंट *n.f.* deodorant
do bār दो बार *adj.* twice (*lit.* "two times")
donoN दोनों *adj.* both
dopahar दोपहर *n.f.* noon
doṣ दोष *n.m.* guilt
drṣṭi दृष्टि *n.f.* sight
drśya दृश्य *n.m.* view (scene)
dubhāṣiyā दुभाषिया *n.m.* interpreter
dūdh दूध *n.m.* milk
dukāndār दुकानदार *n.m.* shopkeeper
dukhī दुखी *adj.* unhappy
dulhan दुल्हन *n.f.* bride
dupaṭṭā दुपट्टा *n.m.* scarf (women's)
dūr दूर *adj.* far

durbhāgyavaś दुर्भाग्यवश *adv.* unfortunately
dūrbīn दूरबीन *n.m.* telescope
dūsrā दूसरा *adj.* another (some other, second)
dūtāvās दूतावास *n.m.* embassy; consulate

E

eḍs एड्स *n.f.* AIDS
ek aur एक और *adj.* another (one more)
ek bār एक बार *adv.* once (one occurrence)
ek minaṭ एक मिनट *n.m.* minute (a)
eks re एक्स रे *n.m.* x-ray
elarjī एलरजी *n.f.* allergy

F

faikṭarī फ़ैक्टरी *n.f.* factory
faislā फ़ैसला *n.m.* decision
farś फ़र्श *n.m.* floor
farz फ़र्ज़ *n.m.* duty
film फ़िल्म *n.f.* film, movie
fītā फ़ीता *n.m.* lace (string)
fon फ़ोन *n.m.* phone
fon karnā फ़ोन करना *v.t.* call (to telephone)
foṭo फ़ोटो *n.m.* photo
foṭogrāfī फ़ोटोग्राफ़ी *n.f.* photography
fuṭbāl फुटबाल *n.m.* soccer

G

gājar गाजर *n.m.* carrot
galā गला *n.m.* throat

galīcā गलीचा *n.m.* rug
gambhīr गंभीर *adj.* serious
gānā गाना *n.m. & v.t.* song; sing (to)
gandā गंदा *adj.* dirty
gānjā गांजा *n.f.* marijuana
gaṇtantra गणतंत्र *n.m.* republic
garabhāśy गर्भाशय *n.m.* uterus
garabhpāt गर्भपात *n.m.* abortion; miscarriage
garabhvatī गर्भवती *n.f.* pregnant
garam गरम *adj.* hot
gāranṭī गॉरंटी *n.f.* guarantee
gaṛbaṛ गड़बड़ *adj. & n.f.* confused; disorder, trouble
gāṛī गाड़ी *n.f.* vehicle; car
garmī गरमी *n.f.* heat; summer
garv गर्व *n.m.* pride
gāNv गाँव *n.m.* village
gavāhī denā गवाही देना *v.t.* testify (to)
gāy (more like gāi) गाय *n.f.* cow
gāyak गायक *n.m.* singer
gāyikā गायिका *n.f.* singer
gehūN गेहूँ *n.m.* wheat
ghar घर *n.m.* home
ghaṛī घड़ी *n.f.* clock
ghās घास *n.f.* grass
ghāṭī घाटी *n.f.* valley
ghāv घाव *n.m.* cut (a wound)
ghoṛā घोड़ा *n.m.* horse
ghrṇā घ्रृणा *n.f.* hatred
ghūs घूस *n.f.* bribe
ghuṭnā घुटना *n.m.* knee

gīlā गीला *adj.* wet
ginnā गिनना *v.t.* count (to)
giraftār karnā गिरफ़्तार करना *v.t.* arrest (to)
girjāghar गिरजाघर *n.m.* church
gol गोल *adj.* round
golā गोला *n.m.* ball
golī गोली *n.f.* pill
gomāNs गोमाँस *n.m.* beef
gorā गोरा *adj.* white (Caucasian)
grah ग्रह *n.m.* planet
grāhak ग्राहक *n.m.* customer
gufā गुफ़ा *n.f.* cave
gulāb गुलाब *n.m.* rose
gulābī गुलाबी *adj.* pink
guṇ गुण *n.m.* quality
gupt rog गुप्त रोग *n.m.* venereal disease (*lit.* "private disease")
gurdā गुर्दा *n.m.* kidney
guruvār गुरुवार *n.m.* Thursday
gusalqhānā गुसलख़ाना *n.m.* bathroom

H

hāN हाँ *adv.* yes
haḍḍī हड्डी *n.f.* bone
haftā हफ़्ता *n.m.* week
haiNḍ baig हैंड बैग *n.m.* handbag
hāl meN हाल में *adv.* recently
ham हम *pron.m.f.* we
hamdard हमदर्द *adj.* sympathetic
hamdardī हमदर्दी *n.f.* sympathy

hameśā हमेशा *adv.* always
hamlā karnā हमला करना *v.t.* attack (to)
harā हरा *adj.* green
har ek हर एक *adj.* each
hariyālī हरियाली *n.f.* vegetation
haṛtāl हड़ताल *n.f.* strike
haNsī हँसी *n.f.* laughter
haNsnā हँसना *v.i.* laugh (to)
haṭānā हटाना *v.t.* take off (to)
hāth हाथ *n.m.* hand
hathauṛā हथौड़ा *n.m.* hammer
hāthī हाथी *n.m.* elephant
haṭhīlā हठीला *adj.* stubborn
hāth kā banā हाथ का बना *adj.* handmade
havā हवा *n.f.* air; wind
havāī aḍḍā हवाई अड्डा *n.f.* airport
havāī ḍāk हवाई डाक *n.f.* air mail
havāī jahāz हवाई जहाज़ *n.m.* airplane
havāī kampanī हवाई कंपनी *n.f.* airline
hicakī हिचकी *n.f.* hiccup
himsā हिंसा *n.f.* violence
hindū हिन्दू *n.m.f.* Hindu
hīrā हीरा *n.m.* diamond
hiran हिरन *n.f.* deer
ho jānā हो जाना *v.i.* become (to); happen (to)
honā होना *v.i.* be (to)
hoNṭh होंठ *n.m.* lips

I

ijāzat इजाज़त *n.f.* permission
ilāqā इलाक़ा *n.m.* region

indradhnuṣ इन्द्रधनुष *n.m.* rainbow
injan इंजन *n.m.* engine
intazār karnā इंतज़ार करना *v.t.* wait (to)
intazār kījiye! इंतज़ार कीजिये *interj.* please wait!
īrṣyālu ईर्ष्यालु *adj.* jealous
īsāī ईसाई *adj. & n.m.f.* Christian
isliye इसलिये *adv.* therefore
istemāl karnā इस्तेमाल करना *v.t.* use (to)
itihās इतिहास *n.m.* history

J

jabaṛā जबड़ा *n.m.* jaw
jab bhī जब भी *adv.* whenever
jab kabhī जब कभी *pron.m.f.* anytime
jādū जादू *n.m.* magic
jādūgar जादूगर *n.m.* magician
jagah जगह *n.f.* space
jagānā जगाना *v.t.* wake up (to wake someone up)
jāgnā जागना *v.i.* wake up (to)
jāgo! जागो *interj.* wake up!
jahāN जहाँ *conj.* where
jahāz जहाज़ *n.m.* ship
jaj जज *n.m.* judge
jākeṭ जाकेट *n.f.* jacket
jalānevālā जलानेवाला *n.m.* lighter (cigarette)
jaldī जल्दी *adv.* early; quickly
jalnā जलना *v.i.* burn (to)
jalvāyu जलवायु *n.m.* climate
jānā जाना *v.i.* go (to)
janamdin जन्मदिन *n.m.* birthday

janampatr जन्मपत्र *n.m.* birth certificate
janam sthān जन्म स्थान *n.m.* place of birth
janasankhyā जनसंख्या *n.f.* population
jān bacānā जान बचाना *v.t.* save (to save a life)
janbhāī जंभाई *n.f.* yawn
janbhāī lenā जंभाई लेना *v.i.* yawn (to)
jānnā जानना *v.t.* know (to know something)
jānvar जानवर *n.m.* animal
jāṛā जाड़ा *n.m.* winter
jāṛī-būṭī जाड़ीक्षबूटी *n.f.* herbs
jāti जाति *n.f.* caste; race (of people)
jātivād जातिवाद *n.m.* racism
javāb जवाब *n.m.* answer
javāb denā जवाब देना *v.t.* answer (to)
javāharāt जवाहरात *n.m.* jewelry
javān जवान *adj.* young
javānī जवानी *n.f.* youth
jayantī जयन्ती *n.f.* anniversary
jeb जेब *n.f.* pocket
jel जेल *n.m.* jail
jelqhānā जेलख़ाना *n.m.* prison
jhagṛā झगड़ा *n.m.* quarrel
jhaṇḍā झण्डा *n.m.* flag
jhapak झपक *n.f.* nap
jharnā झरना *n.m.* waterfall
jhāṛū झाड़ू *n.m.* broom
jhīl झील *n.f.* lake
jhūṭh झूठ *n.m.* lie (falsehood)
jhūṭhā झूठा *n.m.* liar
jhūṭh bolnā झूठ बोलना *v.i. & v.t.* lie (to)
jīnā जीना *v.t.* live (to exist)

jītnā जीतना *v.t.* win (to)
jīvan जीवन *n.m.* life
jīvanī जीवनी *n.f.* biography
jīvan star जीवन स्तर *n.m.* standard of living
jīvit जीवित *adj.* alive
jīvit rehnā जीवित रहना *v.i.* survive (to)
jo bhī जो भी *adv.* whatever
jokhim जोखिम *n.f.* risk
jueN जुएँ *n.f.* lice
juṛvāN जुड़वाँ *n.m.* twins
jūtā जूता *n.m.* shoe
jūte kī dūkhān जूते की दूखान *n.f.* shoe store

K

kab कब *adj. & adv.* when
kabhī kabhī कभी कभी *adj. & adv.* sometimes; occasionally
kabhī nahīN कभी नहीं *adv.* never
kaccā कच्चा *adj.* raw (uncooked)
kāfī काफ़ी *adj.* enough (adequate)
kagār कगार *n.f.* ledge
kahāN कहाँ *adv.* where
kahānī कहानी *n.f.* story
kahīN कहीं *adv.* somewhere
kahīN bhī कहीं भी *adv.* anywhere; wherever
kahīN nahīN कहीं नहीं *adv.* nowhere
kaī कई *adj.* several
kaimarā कैमरा *n.m.* camera
kaise कैसे *adv.* how
kakṣā कक्षा *n.f.* class (school)

kal कल *n.m.* tomorrow; yesterday
kālā काला *adj.* black
kalā कला *n.f.* art
kalākār कलाकर *n.m.* artist
kālej कालेज *n.m.* college
kālī mirc काली मिर्च *n.f.* pepper (black)
kalpanā कल्पना *v.t.* imagine (to)
kam कम *adj.* less
kām काम *n.m.* work
kāma काम *n.m.* pleasure (sensual)
kamānā कमाना *v.t.* earn (to)
kambal कम्बल *n.m.* blanket
kamī कमी *n.f.* shortage
kamīz कमीज़ *n.f.* shirt
kām karnā काम करना *v.t.* work (to)
kampyūṭar कंप्यूटर *n.f.* computer
kamrā कमरा *n.m.* room
kamrā kā nambar कमरा का नंबर *n.m.* room number
kamzor कमज़ोर *adj.* weak
kamzorī कमज़ोरी *n.f.* weakness
kān कान *n.m.* ear
kandhā कंधा *n.m.* shoulder
kanfarm karnā कनफ़र्म करना *v.t.* confirm (to)
kangan कंगन *n.m.* bracelet
kanghī कंघी *n.f.* comb
kaṇṭhī कंठी *n.f.* necklace
kāpī कापी *n.f.* notebook
kapṛa कपड़ा *n.m.* cloth
kapṛe कपड़े *n.m.* clothing
kāqgaz कागज़ *n.m.* paper

kar कर *n.m.* tax
kaṛā कड़ा *adj.* hard
karamcārī कर्मचारी *n.m.f.* employee
kāraṇ कारण *n.m.* reason (cause)
kārḍ कार्ड *n.m.* card
karnā करना *v.t.* do (to)
kārykram कार्यक्रम *n.m.* program
karz कर्ज़ *n.m.* debt
kasarat कसरत *n.f.* exercise
kāṭanā काटना *v.t.* cut (to)
katarnī कतरनी *n.f.* scissors
kaṭu कटु *adj.* bitter
kāufī कौफ़ी *n.f.* coffee
kaun कौन *adj. & pron.m.f.* which; who
kāvya काव्य *n.m.* poetry
kesar केसर *n.m.* saffron
keval केवल *adj. & adv.* just (only)
khamīr खमीर *n.m.* yeast
khānā खाना *n.m. & v.t.* food; eat (to)
khanḍahar खंडहर *n.m.* ruins
kharīdārī karnā खरीदारी करना *v.i.* shop (to go shopping)
kharīdnā खरीदना *v.t.* buy (to)
khāNsī खाँसी *n.f.* cough (a)
khaṭkhṭānā खटखटाना *v.t.* knock (to)
khaṭṭā खट्टा *adj.* sour
khel खेल *n.m.* game
khet खेत *n.m.* field (agricultural), farm
khīrā खीरा *n.m.* cucumber
khiṛkī खिड़की *n.f.* window
khoj karnā खोज करना *v.t.* discover (to)

kholnā खोलना *v.t.* open (to)
khonā खोना *v.t.* lose (to)
khujlī खुजली *n.f.* itch
khulā खुला *adj.* open
khuśbū खुशबू *n.f.* smell (good)
ki कि *conj.* that
kīcaṛ कीचड़ *n.m.* mud
kīl कील *n.f.* nail (hardware)
kilogrām किलोग्राम *n.m.* kilogram
kilomīṭar किलोमीटर *n.m.* kilometer
kīṛā कीड़ा *n.m.* worm; bug
kirāye par lenā किराये पर लेना *v.t.* rent (to)
kisān किसान *n.m.* farmer
kiśmiś किशमिश *n.f.* raisin
kitāb किताब *n.f.* book
kitāb kī dukān किताब की दुकान *n.f.* bookstore
koī कोई *adj. & pron.m.f.* any; somebody
koī bhī कोई भी *pron.m.f.* anyone
koī bhī nahīN कोई भी नहीं *pron.m.f.* none
koī nahīN कोई नहीं *pron.m.f.* nobody
komal कोमल *adj.* delicate
konā कोना *n.m.* corner
koṇḍom कोंडोम *n.m.* condom
koṣ खोष *n.m.* dictionary
kośiś karnā कोशिश करना *v.t.* try (to attempt)
kripālu कृपालु *adj.* kind
kripayā कृपया *adv.* please
kṣāmā karnā क्षमा करना *v.t.* forgive (to)
kṣamā yācanā क्षमा याचना *n.f.* apology
kuch कुछ *adj. & pron.m.f.* few (some); something

kuch bhī कुछ भी *pron.m.f.* anything
kuch nahīN कुछ नहीं *adv.* nothing
kūdnā कूदना *v.i.* jump (to)
kuharā कुहरा *n.m.* fog
kumhārī कुम्हारी *n.f.* pottery
kunain कुनैन *n.f.* quinine
kūṛā कूड़ा *n.m.* garbage
kursī कुर्सी *n.f.* seat (chair)
kursī kī peṭī कुर्सी की पेटी *n.f.* seatbelt
kurtī कुरती *n.f.* blouse
kuttā कुत्ता *n.m.* dog
kyā क्या *interr.* what
kyoN क्यों *interr.* why
kyoNki क्योंकि *conj.* because

L

lābh लाभ *n.m.* profit
lagbhag लगभग *adv.* almost
lahar लहर *n.m.* wave
lāin लाइन *n.f.* line (queue)
lakṛī लकड़ी *n.f.* wood
lakshy लक्ष्य *n.m.* goal; target
lāl लाल *adj.* red
lāl mirc लाल मिर्च *n.f.* pepper (red)
lālṭen लालटेन *n.f.* lantern
lambā लम्बा *adj.* long; tall
lānā लाना *v.t.* bring (to)
laṛāī लड़ाई *n.f.* fight
laṛākā लड़ाका *adj.* aggressive
laṛkā लड़का *n.m.* boy

laṛkī लड़की *n.f.* girl
lāś लाश *n.f.* corpse
lauṭānā लौटाना *v.t.* refund (to)
lauṭnā लौटना *v.i.* return (to)
le jānā ले जाना *v.t.* take (to take away)
lehsun लहसुन *n.m.* garlic
lekhak लेखक *n.m.* writer
lekin लेकिन *conj.* but
lens लेन्स *n.m.* lens
lifāfā लिफ़ाफा *n.m.* envelope
likhnā लिखना *v.t.* write (to)
ling लिंग *n.m.* sex (gender); penis
lipi लिपि *n.f.* script (language)
log लोग *n.m.* people
lokpriya लोकप्रिय *adj.* popular
loktantra लोकतंत्र *n.m.* democracy

M

macchar मच्छडर *n.m.* mosquito
machlī मछली *n.f.* fish
madad मदद *n.f.* help
madad karnā मदद करना *v.t.* help (to)
madhu मधु *n.m.* honey
madhumeha मधुमेह *n.m.* diabetes
madhumehī मधुमेही *adj.* diabetic
madhyak मध्यक *adj.* average
madyarātri मध्यरात्रि *n.f.* midnight
māf karnā माफ़ करना *v.t.* forgive (to)
māf kījiye! माफ़ कीजिये *interj.* excuse me! (*lit.* "forgive me!")

mahaNgā महँगा *adj.* expensive
mahal महल *n.m.* palace
mahāsāgar महासागर *n.m.* ocean
mahasūs karnā महसूस करना *v.i. & v.t.* feel (to experience)
mahatvapūrṇ महत्त्वपूर्ण *adj.* important
māhavārī माहवारी *n.f.* menstruation
mahīnā महीना *n.m.* month
maiN मैं *pron.m.f.* I
maikenik मैकेनिक *n.m.* mechanic
mainejar मैनेजर *n.m.* manager
makkhan मक्खन *n.m.* butter
makkhī मक्खी *n.f.* fly
makṛī मकड़ी *n.f.* spider
malāī मलाई *n.f.* cream
mālik मालिक *n.m.* owner
māliś मालिश *n.f.* massage
māmūlī मामूली *adj.* ordinary
man मन *n.m.* mind
manānā मनाना *v.i. & v.t.* celebrate (to)
mānav मानव *n.m.* human
mānav adhikār मानव अधिकार *n.m.* human rights
mandir मंदिर *n.m.* temple
mangalvār मंगलवार *n.m.* Tuesday
mangetar मंगेतर *n.m.f.* fiancé; fiancée
maṇi मणि *n.f.* jewel
manohār मनोहार *adj.* handsome; charming
manoranjan मनोरंजन *n.m.* entertainment
manpasand मनपसंद *adj.* favorite
mānsik मानसिक *adj.* mental
mānsik bīmārī मानसिक बीमारी *n.f.* mental illness

mānspeśī मांसपेशी *n.f.* muscle
mansūkhī मनसूखी *n.f.* cancellation
manzil मंज़िल *n.f.* destination
marā huā मरा हुआ *adj.* dead
mār ḍālnā मार डालना *v.t.* kill (to)
mārg मार्ग *n.m.* avenue
marnā मरना *v.i.* die (to)
mārnā मारना *v.t.* hit (to)
martabān मर्तबान *n.m.* jar
māNs मांस *n.m.* meat
masāle मसाले *n.m.* spices
masāledār मसालेदार *adj.* spicy (flavorful)
māsik kā dard मासिक का दर्द *n.m.* period (menstrual) pain
maśīn मशीन *n.f.* machine
masjid मसजिद *n.f.* mosque
mastī मस्ती *n.f.* intoxication (from life); delight; unrestrained joy
mastī soyeN! मस्ती सोयें *interj.* sleep well!
mātā-jī माता-जी *n.f.* mother
mātā-pitā माता-पिता *n.m.* parents
maṭh मठ *n.m.* monastery
mathibhram मथिभ्रम *n.m.* hallucination
maṭhvāsinī मठवासिनी *n.f.* nun
maulavī मौलवी *n.m.* priest (Muslim)
mausam मौसम *n.m.* weather
mazā मज़ा *adj.* fun
mazā ānā मज़ा आना *v.t.* fun (to have)
mazāk मज़ाक *n.m.* joke
mazāk karnā मज़ाक करना *v.i.* joke (to)
… meN … में *post.* inside; among

mehamān मेहमान *n.m.f.* guest
mehsūl महसूल *n.m.* postage
menyū मेन्यू *n.m.* menu
merā मेरा *pron.m.s.* my (object determines gender and number)
mere मेरे *pron.m.pl.* my (object determines gender and number)
merī मेरी *pron.f.s.pl.* my (object determines gender and number)
mez मेज़ *n.f.* table
miclī मिचली *n.f.* nausea
mijāz मिजाज़ *n.f.* mood
milnā मिलना *v.i.* meet (to)
milne jānā मिलने जाना *v.i.* visit (to)
mīnār मीनार *n.f.* tower
minaral vāṭar मिनरल वॉटर *n.m.* water (mineral)
mirc मिर्च *n.f.* chili pepper
mirgī kā rogī मिरगी का रोगी *n.m.* epileptic
mīṭhā मीठा *adj.* sweet
miṭhāī मिठाई *n.f.* sweet (candy)
mombattī मोमबत्ती *n.f.* candle
moṭā मोटा *adj.* fat; thick
moṭar saikil मोटर साइकिल *n.f.* motorcycle
mozā मोज़ा *n.m.* sock
mrityu मृत्यू *n.f.* death
muft मुफ़्त *adj.* free (no charge)
mūNgfalī मूँगफ़ली *n.f.* peanut
muNh मुँह *n.m.* face; mouth
muhabbat मुहब्बत *n.f.* love
muhallā मुहल्ला *n.m.* suburb
mukhya मुख्य *adj.* chief

mūl मूल *adj.* original
mulāyam मुलायम *adj.* soft
mūlī मूली *n.f.* radish
mūlyvān मूल्यवान *adj.* valuable
murdā मुरदा *adj.* dead
murgī मुर्गी *n.f.* chicken
mūrkh मूर्ख *adj.* stupid (foolish)
mūNṛnā मूँड़ना *v.t.* shave (to)
mūrtī मूर्ती *n.f.* statue
mūrtikalā मूर्तिकला *n.f.* sculpture
mūrtikār मूर्तिकार *n.m.* sculptor
musalmān मुसलमान *n.m.* Muslim
musalmanī मुसलमानी *adj.* Muslim
muskarāhaṭ मुस्कराहट *n.f.* smile
muskarānā मुस्कराना *v.t.* smile (to)
muśkil मुश्किल *v.t.* smile (to)

N

nācnā नाचना *v.i.* dance
nadī नदी *n.f.* river
nagar नगर *n.m.* town
nāgarik नागरिक *n.m.* citizen
nāgarik adhikār नागरिक अधिकार *n.m.* rights (civil)
nāgariktā नागरिकता *n.f.* citizenship
nahānā नहाना *v.i.* wash (to bathe oneself)
nahīN नहीं *adv.* no
naipkin नैपकिन *n.f.* napkin
nāk नाक *n.f.* nose
nakh नख *n.m.* nail (of person)
nām नाम *n.m.* name

namak नमक *n.m.* salt
namaskār / namaste नमस्कार *for.* / नमस्ते *inf.* hello (also used for good-bye)
nānā नाना *n.f.* grandfather (maternal)
nangā नंगा *adj.* naked
nānī नानी *n.f.* grandmother (maternal)
naqlī नक़ली *n.f.* artificial
naqśā नक़्शा *n.m.* map
nārangī नारंगी *adj.* orange (color)
narāz नराज़ *adj.* angry
nars नर्स *n.f.* nurse
naśā नशा *n.m.* intoxication (from substance)
naśā caṛhanā नशा चढ़ना *v.i.* drunk (to be)
naśe meN नशे में *adj.* stoned (from drugs)
nāśtā नाश्ता *n.m.* breakfast
nāṭak नाटक *n.m.* drama (a play)
naukrī नौकरी *n.f.* job
nāv नाव *n.f.* boat
navvarṣ नववर्ष *n.m.* New Year's Day
nayā नया *adj.* new
nāzuk नाज़ुक *adj.* fragile
netā नेता *n.m.* leader
nībū नीबू *n.m.* lemon
nicalā निचला *adj.* bottom
nīce नीचे *adv.* below, under
nideśikā निदेशिका *n.f.* directory
nigalnā निगलना *v.t.* swallow (to)
nikās निकास *n.m.* exit
nīlā नीला *adj.* blue
nimantraṇ निमंत्रण *n.m.* invitation
nīnd नींद *n.f.* sleep

nīnd ānā नींद आना *v.i.* sleepy (to feel)
nirāśā निराशा *n.f.* disappointment
nirmāṇ निर्माण *n.m.* construction
nirodhak निरोधक *n.m.* contraceptive
niśānī निशानी *n.f.* souvenir
niścay karnā निश्चय *v.t.* decide (to)
niścit निश्चित *adj.* sure (certain)
nivās निवास *n.m.* residence
niyam नियम *n.m.* rule (regulation)
niyati नियति *n.f.* destiny
niyojan नियोजन *n.m.* appointment
nusqhā नुसख़ा *n.m.* prescription (medical)
nyāy न्याय *n.m.* justice

P

pachtānā पछताना *v.t.* regret (to)
padak पदक *n.m.* medal
pādrī पादरी *n.m.* priest (Christian)
pāgal पागल *adj.* crazy
pahacānnā पहचानना *v.t.* recognize (to)
pahalā पहला *n.m.* first
pahale पहले *adv.* before (earlier)
pahāṛ पहाड़ *n.m.* mountain
pahāṛī पहाड़ी *n.f.* hill
pahicān पहिचान *n.f.* identification
pahuNcanā पहुँचना *v.i.* arrive (to)
paidal jānā पैदल जाना *v.i.* walk (to)
paidal sair karnā पैदल सैर करना *v.i. & v.t.* hike
pair पैर *n.m.* foot
paisā पैसा *n.m.* money

paise denā पैसे देना *v.t.* to pay (money)
pakānā पकाना *v.t.* cook (to)
pālak पालक *n.m.* spinach
pānā पाना *v.t.* find (to); get (to); obtain (to)
panchāng पंचांग *n.m.* calendar
pānī पानी *n.m.* water
panīr पनीर *n.m.* cheese
pankha पंख *n.m.* wing; fan
pannā पन्ना *n.m.* page (of book, etc.)
pāp पाप *n.m.* sin
pāp karnā पाप करना *v.t.* sin (to)
par पर *prep.* on
paramāṇu ūrjā परमाणु ऊर्जा *n.f.* nuclear energy
paramparā परम्परा *n.f.* tradition
pāramparik पारम्परिक *adj.* traditional
pardā परदा *n.m.* screen; veil
pareśānī परेशानी *n.f.* harassment
paṛhnā पढ़ना *v.t.* read (to)
paricay परिचय *n.m.* introduction
paricay denā परिचय देना *v.t.* introduce (to)
parīkṣā परीक्षा *n.f.* examination (school)
parivahan परिवहन *n.m.* transportation
parivār परिवार *n.m.* family
parivār kā nām परिवार का नाम *n.m.* surname (last name)
pārk पार्क *n.m.* park
paṛosī पड़ोसी *n.m.* neighbor
pārsal पार्सल *n.m.* package (parcel)
pārṭī पार्टी *n.f.* party
parvāh karnā परवा करना *v.t.* care (to take interest)
paryṭak पर्यटक *n.m.* tourist

pās पास *adv.* near
pasand karnā पसंद करना *v.t.* to enjoy
paścim पश्चिम *n.m.* West
pasīnā bahānā पसीना बहाना *v.i.* perspire (to)
pāsporṭ पासपोर्ट *n.m.* passport
pāsport nambar पासपोर्ट नबंर *n.m.* passport number
patā पता *n.m.* address
patā lagānā पता लगाना *v.i. & v.t.* discover; find out (to)
path पथ *n.m.* trail (path)
pati पति *n.m.* husband
patlā पतला *adj.* thin
patlūn पतलून *n.m.* pants
patnī पत्नी *n.f.* wife
patrakār पत्रकार *n.m.* journalist
patrikā पत्रिका *n.f.* magazine (periodical)
pattā पत्ता *n.m.* leaf
patthar पत्थर *n.m.* stone
paṭṭī पट्टी *n.f.* bandage
paudhā पौधा *n.m.* plant
pavitr पवित्र *adj.* sacred
pāylaṭ पायलट *n.m.* pilot
pehennā पहनना *v.t.* wear (to)
pensil पेंसिल *n.f.* pencil
peṛ पेड़ *n.m.* tree
peśā पेशा *n.m.* occupation
peśāb karnā पेशाब करना *v.t.* urinate (to)
peṭ पेट *n.m.* stomach
peṭ kā dard पेट का दर्द *n.m.* stomachache
peṭrol पेट्रोल *n.m.* petrol, fuel (gas)
phal फल *n.m.* fruit

phapholā फफोला *n.m.* blister
phephaṛā फेफड़ा *n.m.* lungs
phir mileNge! फिर मिलेंगे *interj.* see you later!
phoṛā फोड़ा *n.m.* ulcer
phuhārā snān karnā फुहारा स्नान करना *v.t.* shower (to take a shower)
phūl फूल *n.m.* flower
pichāṛī पिछाड़ी *n.f.* rear
pīche पीछे *adv.* behind
pīche-pīche calnā पीछे-पीछे चलना *v.i. & v.t.* follow (to)
pichlā पिछला *adj.* last (previous)
pickārī पिचकारी *n.f.* syringe
pīnā पीना *v.i. & v.t.* drink (to)
pin koḍ पिन कोड *n.m.* postal code (zip code)
pīr पीर *n.m.* saint (Muslim)
pissū पिस्सू *n.m.* flea
pitā-jī पिता-जी *n.m.* father
pīṭh पीठ *n.f.* back (of body)
pīṭh kā dard पीठ का दर्द *n.m.* backache
plāsṭik प्लास्टिक *n.f.* plastic
pleṭ प्लेट *n.m.* plate
pleṭfārm प्लेटफ़ार्म *n.m.* platform
posṭ-kārḍ पोस्ट-कार्ड *n.m.* postcard
potaṛā kaloṭ पोतड़ा कलोट *n.m.* diaper
poṭlā पोटला *n.m.* pack; large bundle
prācīn प्राचीन *adj.* ancient
pradhān mantrī प्रधान मंत्री *n.m.f.* prime minister
pradūṣaṇ प्रदूषण *n.m.* pollution
prakriti प्रकृति *n.f.* nature (of the Earth, etc.)
prākritik प्राकृतिक *adj.* natural (of the Earth, etc.)

pralekhan प्रलेखन *n.m.* documentation
pramāṇ-patr प्रमाण-पत्र *n.m.* certificate
praṇām प्रणाम *interj. & n.m.* respectful greetings!; respectful greeting
prāpt karnā प्राप्त करना *v.t.* receive (to)
prārthnā प्रार्थना *n.f.* prayer
prārthnā karnā प्रार्थना करना *v.t.* pray (to)
praśānt mahāsāgar प्रशान्त महासागर *n.m.* Pacific Ocean
prasāraṇ प्रसारण *n.m.* radio broadcast
prasiddh प्रसिद्ध *adj.* famous
prastāv प्रस्ताव *n.m.* proposal
praṣṭh प्रष्ठ *n.m.* page
prasthān प्रस्थान *n.m.* departure
prastutīkaraṇ प्रस्तुतीकरण *n.f.* presentation
pratibhāśālī प्रतिभाशाली *adj.* talented
pratijaiviki प्रतिजैविकि *n.f.* antibiotic
pratīk प्रतीक *n.m.* symbol
pratīkshālay प्रतीक्षालय *n.m.* transit lounge
pratirakṣīkaraṇ प्रतिरक्षीकरण *n.m.* immunization
pratiśat प्रतिशत *n.m.* percent
praveś प्रवेश *n.m.* entrance
praveś karnā प्रवेश करना *v.i. & v.t.* enter (to)
prayog प्रयोग *n.m.* use
prem प्रेम *n.m.* love
premī प्रेमी *n.m.* lover
premikā प्रेमिका *n.f.* lover
pres karnā प्रेस करना *v.t.* iron (to press)
prkāś प्रकाश *n.m.* light
projekṭar प्रोजेकटर *n.m.* projector
pūchnā पूछना *v.t.* question (to)

pūjā karnā पूजा करना *v.t.* worship (to)
pujārī पुजारी *n.m.* priest (Hindu)
pul पुल *n.m.* bridge
pulis पुलिस *n.f.* police
pūrā पूरा *adj.* whole (all)
purānā पुराना *adj.* old (thing)
purātattva पुरातत्त्व *n.m.* archaeology
purāvastu पुरावसतु *n.f.* antique
pūrṇ पूर्ण *adj.* full
pūrva पूर्व *n.m.* East
pustakālay पुस्तकालय *n.m.* library
pūtirodhī पूतिरोधी *n.f.* antiseptic
pyālā प्याला *n.m.* cup
pyār प्यार *n.m.* love
pyār karnā प्यार करना *v.t.* love (to)
pyās lagnā प्यास लगना *v.i.* thirsty (to be)
pyāz प्याज़ *n.m.* onion

Q

qabz क़ब्ज़ *n.f.* constipation
qadam क़दम *n.m.* step (footstep)
qalam क़लम *n.f.* pen
qānūn क़ानून *n.m.* law
qānūnī क़ानूनी *adj.* legal
qgalat ग़लत *adj.* wrong
qgaltī ग़लती *n.f.* fault (guilt)
qgarīb ग़रीब *adj.* poor
qgarībī ग़रीबी *n.f.* poverty
qgussā गुस्सा *adj.* mad (angry)
qhabardār! ख़बरदार *interj.* beware!

qhālī ख़ाली *adj.* empty, vacant
qharab ख़राब *adj.* bad
qhargoś ख़रगोश *n.m.* rabbit
qhas taur se ख़ास तौर से *adv.* especially
qhatara ख़तरा *n.m.* danger
qhatarnāk ख़तरनाक *adj.* dangerous
qhazāncī ख़ज़ांची *n.f.* cashier
qhūn खून *n.m.* blood
qhūn kī jāNc खून की जाँच *n.f.* blood test
qhūn nikalnā खून निकलना *v.i.* bleed (to)
qhuś खुश *adj.* happy
qhuśī खुशी *n.f.* happiness

R

radd karnā रद्द करना *v.t.* cancel (to)
railī रैली *n.f.* rally
rājā राजा *n.m.* king
rājbhavan राजभवन *n.m.* palace
rājdhānī राजधानी *n.f.* capital
rājdūt राजदूत *n.m.* ambassador
rājnayik राजनयिक *n.m.* diplomat
rājnīti राजनीति *n.f.* politics
rājnītigya राजनीतिज्ञ *n.m.* politician
rākhdānī राखदानी *n.f.* ashtray
rakhnā रखना *v.i. & v.t.* keep (to); put (to)
rakshā karnā रक्षा करना *v.t.* protect (to)
raktacāp रक्तचाप *n.m.* blood pressure
rang रंग *n.m.* dye; color
rānī रानी *n.f.* queen
ras रस *n.m.* juice

rāśi cakra राशि चक्र *n.f.* zodiac
rasīd रसीद *n.f.* receipt
rasoīghar रसोईघर *n.m.* kitchen
rastā रास्ता *n.m.* way (path)
rāṣṭra राष्ट्र *n.m.* nation
rāṣṭrapati राष्ट्रपति *n.m.* president (of a country)
rāṣṭriy राष्ट्रिय *adj.* national
rāṣṭriyatā राष्ट्रियता *n.f.* nationality
rāt रात *n.f.* night
rāt kā khānā रात का खाना *n.m.* dinner
ravānā honā रवाना होना *v.i.* depart (to)
ravivār रविवार *n.m.* Sunday
ray (more like rai) राय *n.f.* opinion
reḍiyeṭar रेडियेटर *n.m.* radiator
registān रेगिस्तान *n.m.* desert
rehnā रहना *v.i.* stay (to); live (to); remain (to)
relgāṛī रेलगाड़ी *n.f.* train
rel sṭeśan रेल स्टेशन *n.m.* train station
relve रेलवे *n.f.* railroad
relve sṭeśan रेलवे स्टेशन *n.m.* train station
reśm रेशम *n.m.* silk
restrāN रेस्तराँ *n.m.* restaurant
rivāz रिवाज़ *n.m.* custom (tradition)
rog रोग *n.m.* disease
rogmukti रोगमुक्ति *n.f.* cure
roknā रोकना *v.i. & v.t.* stop (to)
rom रोम *n.m.* hair (of body)
rozānā रोज़ाना *adj.* daily
rumāl रुमाल *n.m.* handkerchief
rūs रूस *n.m.* Russia
rūsī रूसी *adj.* Russian

S

sab सब *adj.* all
śabd शब्द *n.m.* word
śabdāvalī शब्दावली *n.f.* vocabulary
sab jagah सब जगह *adv.* everywhere
sab kuch सब कुछ *pron.m.f.* everything
sabse acchā सबसे अचछा *adj.* the best
sābun साबुन *n.m.* soap
sabzī सब्ज़ी *n.f.* vegetable
saccāī सच्चाई *n.f.* truth
sādā सादा *adj.* plain
sadā ke liye सदा के लिये *adv.* forever
sadasya सदस्य *n.m.* member
śādī शादी *n.f.* marriage; wedding
śādī karnā शादी करना *v.t.* marry (to)
sāf साफ़ *adj.* clean
safāī सफ़ाई *n.f.* cleaning
safed सफ़ेद *adj.* white
sagāī सगाई *n.f.* engagement
sahamat honā सहमत होना *v.i. & v.t.* agree (to)
sahamati सहमति *n.f.* agreement
sahanā सहना *v.i.* suffer; endure (to)
śahar शहर *n.m.* city
sahārā denā सहारा देना *v.t.* support (to)
sahī सही *adj.* true
sahyog सहयोग *n.m.* participation
sāikil साइकिल *n.f.* bicycle
sāikil calānā साइकिल चलाना *v.i.* cycle (to)
śailī शैली *n.f.* style
sair सैर *n.f.* tour
śākāhārī शाकाहारी *adj. & n.m.* vegetarian

śākāhārī khānā शाकाहारी खाना *n.m.* vegetarian food
śākhā शाखा *n.f.* branch (of business)
saknā सकना *v.aux.* can (to be able to)
śakti शक्ति *n.f.* power
sāl साल *n.m.* year
salāh सलाह *n.f.* advice
śām शाम *n.f.* evening
samācār समाचार *n.m.* news
samācārpatr समाचारपत्र *n.m.* newspaper
samāj समाज *n.m.* society
samajhnā समझना *v.t.* understand (to)
sāmājik vigyān सामाजिक विज्ञान *n.m.* social science
samājvād समाजवाद *n.m.* socialism
samājvādī समाजवादी *adj. & n.m.* socialist
samān समान *adj.* same; similar
sāmān सामान *n.m.* baggage
samāntā समानता *n.f.* similarity
samāroh समारोह *n.m.* celebration
samasyā समस्या *n.f.* problem
samatal समतल *adj.* flat
samay समय *n.m.* time
samay par समय पर *adj. & adv.* on time
samay sāriṇī समय सारिणी *n.f.* timetable
sambandh सम्बन्ध *n.m.* connection (relation)
sambhav संभव *adj.* possible
samīkshā समिक्षा *n.f.* review (literary)
śāmil karnā शामिल करना *v.t.* include (to)
samlingkāmī समलिंगकामी *adj.* homosexual
samlingkāmuktā समलिंगकामुकता *n.f.* homosexuality

sammān सम्मान *n.m.* honor
sāmne kā सामने का *adj.* opposite
sampādak संपादक *n.m.* editor
samudr समुद्र *n.m.* sea
samudr taṭ समुद्र तट *n.m.* seashore
samūh समूह *n.m.* group
sāmyavādī साम्यवादी *adj. & n.m.* communist
sanbhog संभोग *n.m.* sexual intercourse
sandeś सन्देश *n.m.* message
sandūk संदूक *n.m.* box
sandūṣaṇ संदूषण *n.m.* infection
sangaṭhan संगठन *n.m.* organization (structure)
sangha संघ *n.m.* union (society)
sangīt संगीत *n.m.* music
sangītkār संगीतकार *n.m.* musician
sangīt samāroh संगीत समारोह *n.m.* concert
sangrahālay संग्रहालय *n.m.* museum
sangrodh संगरोध *n.m.* quarantine
śani शनि *n.m.* Saturn
śanivār शनिवार *n.m.* Saturday
sankaṭ संकट *n.m.* emergency, crisis
sanket संकेत *n.m.* sign
sankhyā संख्या *n.m.* number
sankoc संकोच *n.m.* modesty
sansad संसद *n.f.* parliament
sansār संसार *n.m.* world
sansthān संस्थान *n.m.* institute
sant संत *n.m.* saint (Hindu)
śānt शान्त *n.m.* quiet
santarā संतरा *n.m.* orange (fruit)
śānti शान्ति *n.f.* peace

śāntipūrṇ शान्तिपूर्ण *adj.* peaceful
santoṣ संतोष *n.m.* satisfaction
santoṣ honā संतोष होना *v.i.* satisfied (to be)
santulit संतुलित *adj.* balanced
sanvidhān संविधान *n.m.* constitution (of a state)
sanyog संयोग *n.m.* chance (coincidence)
sāNp साँप *n.m.* snake
saphal सफल *adj.* successful
saphaltā सफलता *n.f.* success
sapnā dekhnā सपना देखना *v.i. & v.t.* dream (to)
śarāb शराब *n.f.* liquor, alcohol
śarad शरद *n.f.* fall (autumn)
saṛak सड़क *n.f.* road, street
saral सरल *adj.* simple
śaraṇārthī शरणार्थी *n.m.* refugee
śarīr शरीर *n.m.* body
sarjan सरजन *n.m.* surgeon
sarkār सरकार *n.f.* government
sarkas सरकस *n.m.* circus
śarmindā honā शरमिंदा होना *v.i.* embarassed (to be)
śastr शस्त्र *n.m.* weapon
śataranj शतरंज *n.m.* chess
śataranj kī basāt शतरंज की बसात *n.f.* chessboard
sāth साथ *prep.* with
sāthī साथी *n.m.* companion
sāth sāth साथ साथ *adv.* together
saubhāgyaśālī सौभाग्यशाली *adj.* lucky
śaucālay शौचालय *n.m.* toilet
savāl सवाल *n.m.* question
sāvdhānī सावधानी *n.f.* caution
sāvdhānī se jāiye! सावधानी से जाइये *interj.* be careful! (*lit.* "go safely!")

saverā सवेरा *n.m.* morning
śāyad शायद *adv.* perhaps
seb सेब *n.m.* apple
senā सेना *n.f.* army; military
śer शेर *n.m.* lion
sevā सेवा *n.f.* service
sīdhā सीधा *adj.* straight
sifāriś सिफ़ारिश *n.f.* recommendation
sifāriś karnā सिफ़ारिश करना *v.t.* recommend (to)
sigreṭ सिग्रेट *n.f.* cigarette
śikār शिकार *n.m.* victim
śikāyat शिकायत *n.f.* complaint
sīkhnā सीखना *v.t.* learn (to)
śikṣā शिक्षा *n.f.* education
silāī karnā सिलाई करना *v.t.* sew (to)
silsilā सिलसिला *n.m.* series
sīmā सीमा *n.f.* border
sinemā सिनेमा *n.m.* cinema
sinha सिंह *n.m.* lion
sipāhī सिपाही *n.m.* soldier
sir सिर *n.m.* head
sir caṛhānā सिर चढ़ाना *v.t.* spoil (to overindulge)
sirdard सिरदर्द *n.m.* headache
sirf सिर्फ़ *adj. & adv.* just (only)
sīṛhī सीढ़ी *n.f.* stairway
śīśā शीशा *n.m.* glass
śiśū शिशू *n.m.* baby
smārak स्मारक *n.m.* monument
snān स्नान *n.m.* bath
snān karnā स्नान करना *v.t.* bathe (to)
socnā सोचना *v.t.* think (to)

śodh शोध *n.m.* research
śodh karnā शोध करना *v.t.* research (to)
śok शोक *n.m.* mourning
somvār सोमवार *n.m.* Monday
sonā सोना *n.m. & v.t.* gold; sleep (to)
sone kā kamrā सोने का कमरा *n.m.* bedroom
śor शोर *n.m.* noise
spaṣṭ स्पष्ट *adj.* clear
spaṣṭ karnā स्पष्ट करना *v.t.* explain (to)
sthān स्थान *n.m.* location (place)
sthānīy स्थानीय *adj.* local
sthāpit karnā स्थापित करना *v.t.* establish (to)
sthāyī स्थायी *adj.* permanent
sthiti स्थिति *n.f.* situation
sūar सूअर *n.m.* pig
śubh rātrī! शुभ रात्री *interj.* good night!
śuddh शुद्ध *adj.* pure
sugandh सुगन्ध *n.f.* perfume
sūNghnā सूँघना *v.i.* smell (to)
sūī सूई *n.f.* needle
sūjan सूजन *n.f.* inflammation
sūkhnā सूखना *v.i. & v.t.* dry (to)
śukriyā! शुक्रिया *interj.inf.* thanks!
sundar सुनदर *adj.* beautiful, pretty
sunnā सुनना *v.i. & v.t.* hear (to); listen (to)
śūnya शून्य *n.m.* zero
surakshā सुरक्षा *n.m.* safety
surakṣit सुरक्षित *adj.* safe
śurūāt शुरूआत *n.f.* beginning
śurū karnā शुरू करना *v.i. & v.t.* begin (to)
sūrya सूर्य *n.m.* sun

sūryāst सूर्यास्त *n.m.* sunset
sūryoday सूर्योदय *n.m.* sunrise
sūtī सूती *n.m.* cotton
sūṭkes सूटकेस *n.m.* suitcase
svabhāv स्वभाव *n.m.* nature (as in human nature)
svābhāvik स्वाभाविक *adj.* natural (of behavior, etc.)
svacālit स्वचालित *adj.* automatic
svād स्वाद *n.m.* taste
svādiṣṭ स्वादिष्ट *adj.* tasty, delicious
svāgatam! स्वागतम *interj.* welcome!
svarg स्वर्ग *n.m.* paradise
svārthī स्वार्थी *adj.* selfish
svatantra स्वतंत्रा *adj.* independent
svatantratā स्वतंत्रता *n.f.* independence; freedom
svayam sevak स्वयं सेवक *n.m.* volunteer
svayam sevā karnā स्वयं सेवा करना *v.t.* volunteer (to)

T

tab तब *adv.* then
tabīyat तबीयत *n.f.* health
ṭāNgnā टाँगना *v.t.* hang (to hang on wall, etc.)
ṭaiksī टैकसी *n.m.* taxi
ṭaiksī sṭaiNḍ टैकसी स्टैंड *n.m.* taxi stand
ṭāileṭ pepar टैलेट पेपर *n.m.* toilet paper
ṭaimpān टैम्पॉन *n.m.* tampon
tairnā तैरना *v.i.* swim (to)
tairne ke kapṛe तैरने के कपड़े *n.m.* swimsuit
taiyār तैयार *adj.* ready
taiyār ho jānā तैयार हो जाना *v.i.* ready (to be)

taiyār karnā तैयार करना *v.t.* prepare (to)
... tak ... तक *post.* until ...
ṭakhnā टखना *n.m.* ankle
takiyā तकिया *n.m.* pillow
takiye kā gilāf तकिये का गिलाफ़ *n.m.* pillowcase
taknīk तकनीक *n.m.* technique
taknīkī तकनीकी *adj.* technical
tāl ताल *n.m.* rhythm
tālā ताला *n.m.* padlock
talā huā तला हुआ *adj.* fried
tālā lagānā ताला लगाना *v.t.* lock (to)
talāq तलाक़ *n.f.* divorce
talnā तलना *v.t.* fry (to)
talvār तलवार *n.f.* sword
tamāśā तमाशा *n.m.* show (spectacle)
tambākū तंबाकू *n.f.* tobacco
tambū तंभू *n.m.* tent
tandurust तंदुरुस्त *adj.* well (healthy)
tang तंग *adj.* narrow; tight
ṭāng टांग *n.m.* leg
tanqhvāh तनख़्वाह *n.f.* salary
tapasvī तपस्वी *n.m.* monk
tāpmān तापमान *n.m.* temperature (outside)
ṭāpū टापू *n.m.* island
tār तार *n.m.* telegram
tārā तारा *n.m.* star
taraf तरफ़ *n.f.* side; direction
tarah tarah तरह तरह *adj.* various
ṭārc टॉर्च *n.m.* flashlight
tārīqh तारीख़ *n.f.* date (calendar day)
tasvīr banānā तस्वीर बनाना *v.t.* paint; draw (to)

tauliyā तौलिया *n.m.* towel
tavā तवा *n.m.* pan
tāzā ताज़ा *adj.* fresh
tel तेल *n.m.* oil
ṭep टेप *n.m.* cassette
tez तेज़ *adj.* fast; loud
thailā थैला *n.m.* bag
thakā huā थका हुआ *adj.* tired (I am)
thaknā थकना *v.i.* tired (to become)
ṭhaṇḍā ठण्डा *adj.* cold
ṭhīk ठीक *adj.* right (correct)
ṭhīk hai! ठीक है *interj.* OK!
ṭhokar mārnā ठोकर मारना *v.t.* kick (to)
thoṛā थोड़ा *adj.* little (a small amount)
ṭhos ठोस *adj.* solid
tijaurī तिजौरी *n.f.* safe; vault
ṭīkā टीका *n.m.* vaccination
ṭīkā lagānā टीका लगाना *v.t.* vaccinate (to)
ṭikaṭ टिकट *n.m.* stamp (postage); ticket
tilcaṭṭā तिलचट्टा *n.m.* cockroach
ṭīm टीम *n.f.* team
ṭin kholne vālā टिन खोल्ने वाला *n.m.* can opener
tīrth-mandir तीथ मंदिर *n.m.* shrine
tīsrā तीसरा *adj.* third
tītā तीता *adj.* spicy (hot)
tohfā तोहफ़ा *n.m.* present (gift)
tolnā तोलना *v.t.* weigh (to)
ṭopī टोपी *n.f.* hat
ṭraival ejenṭ ट्रैवल एजेंट *n.m.* travel agency
ṭrak ट्रक *n.m.* truck
tūfān तूफ़ान *n.m.* storm

ṭukṛā टुकड़ा *n.m.* piece
tulsī तुलसी *n.f.* basil
tum तुम *pron.fam.m.f.* you
ṭūṭā huā टूटा हुआ *adj.* broken
ṭūṭe paise टूटे पैसे *n.m.* change (coins)
ṭuth braś टुथ ब्रश *n.m.* toothbrush
ṭūṭnā टूटना *v.t.* break (to)
tyohār त्योहार *n.m.* holiday (celebrated day)

U

ūbā huā *m.* / **huī** *f.* ऊबा हुआ *adj.m.* / हुई *adj.f.* bored
ubāū उबाऊ *adj.* boring
ūNcā ऊँचा *adj.* high
ūNcāī ऊँचाई *n.f.* height, altitude
udāharaṇ उदाहरण *n.m.* example
udārtā उदारता *n.f.* generosity
udās उदास *adj.* sad
udāsī उदासी *n.f.* sadness
udhār उधार *n.m.* loan
udhār lenā उधार लेना *v.t.* borrow (to)
ulkā उल्का *n.f.* meteor
ulṭī उलटी *n.f.* vomit
ulṭī honā उलटी होना *v.i.* vomit (to)
umas उमस *n.m.* humidity (heat)
ūn ऊन *n.m.* wool
upādhi उपाधि *n.f.* degree (college)
upahār उपहार *n.m.* present (gift)
upanyās उपन्यास *n.m.* novel (type of book)
ūpar ऊपर *adv.* up

upnagar उपनगर *n.m.* suburb
upyogī उपयोगी *adj.* useful
uṛān उड़ान *n.f.* flight
uṛnā उड़ना *v.i.* fly (to)
uṣā-kāl उषा-काल *n.m.* dawn
ustarā उस्तरा *n.m.* razor
utsav उत्सव *n.m.* festival
uttar उश्वर *adj. & n.m.* North

V

vādā वादा *n.m.* promise
vafādār वफ़ादार *adj.* loyal
vahāN (wahāN) वहाँ *adv.* there
vaidhīkaraṇ वैधीकरण *n.m.* legalization
vāiras वाइरस *n.m.* virus
vakīl वकील *n.m.* lawyer
vākya वाक्य *n.m.* sentence (grammatical)
van वन *n.m.* forest
vānaspatik वानस्पतिक *adj.* botanical
varg वर्ग *n.m.* class (social)
vasant वसंत *n.m.* spring (season)
vāstukalā वास्तुकला *n.f.* architecture
vāstukār वास्तुकार *n.m.* architect
vātāvaraṇ वातावरण *n.m.* atmosphere (environment)
ve वे *pron.m.f.pl.* these/they (he/she/it *pl.* and *s.for.*)
vhīl caiyar व्हील चैयर *n.m.* wheelchair
vibhāg विभाग *n.m.* department
vicār विचार *n.m.* thought
vicār karnā विचार करना *v.t.* discuss (to)

vicār-vimarś विचार-विमर्श *n.m.* discussion
vicched विच्छेद *n.m.* separation
videśī विदेशी *adj. & n.m.* foreign; foreigner
videśī dveṣ विदेशी द्वेष *n.m.* xenophobia
vidhvā विधवा *n.f.* widow
vidyālay विद्यालय *n.m.* school
vidyārthī विद्यार्थी *n.m.* student
vigyān विज्ञान *n.m.* science
vigyānī विग्यानी *n.m.* scientist
vijetā विजेता *n.m.* winner
viklāṅg विकलांग *adj.* disabled, handicapped
vilās विलास *n.m.* sensual pleasure
vimān विमान *n.m.* airplane
vinimay kī dar विनिमय की दर *n.f.* exchange rate
viral विरल *adj.* rare (infrequent)
virodh विरोध *n.m.* protest
virodh karnā विरोध करना *v.t.* object, protest (to)
viṣailā विषैला *adj.* toxic; poisonous
viśeṣagy विशेषज्ञ *n.m.* specialist
viśva विश्व *n.m.* universe
viśvās विश्वास *n.m.* belief, confidence
viśvās karnā विश्वास करना *v.t.* believe (to)
viśvavidyālay विश्वविद्यालय *n.m.* university
vīzā वीज़ा *n.m.* visa
voh वह *pron.m.f.s.* that/he/she/it
voṭ denā वोट देना *v.t.* vote (to)
vyākaraṇ व्याकरण *n.m.* grammar
vyakti व्यक्ति *n.m.* person
vyaktigat व्यक्तिगत *adj.* private (personal)
vyaktitva व्यक्तित्व *n.m.* personality
vyāpār व्यापार *n.m.* business

vyasan व्यसन *n.m.* addiction
vyast व्यस्त *adj.* busy; occupied
vyavasāy व्यवसाय *n.m.* profession

Y

yā या *conj.* or
yād याद *n.f.* memory; remembrance
yadi यदि *conj.* if
yād karnā याद करना *v.t.* remember (to)
yāgya यज्ञ *n.m.* sacrifice (rite)
yahāN यहाँ *adv.* here
yahūdī यहूदी *adj.* Jewish
yahūdiyoN kā mandir यहूदियों का मंदिर *n.m.* synagogue
yātāyāt यातायात *n.m.* traffic
yātrā यात्रा *n.f.* journey
yātrā karnā यात्रा करना *v.t.* travel (to)
yātrākram यात्राक्रम *n.m.* itinerary
yātrī यात्री *n.m.* passenger
ye ये *pron.m.f.pl.* these/they (he/she/it *pl.* and *s.for.*)
yeh यह *pron.m.f.s.* this/he/she/it
yogyatā योग्यता *n.f.* qualifications
yojnā योजना *n.f.* plan
yoni योनि *n.f.* vagina

Z

zahar ज़हर *n.m.* poison
zaitūn ज़ैतून *n.m.* olive

zarūrī ज़रूरी *adj.* urgent; necessary
zebrā ज़ेबरा *n.m.* zebra
zindā ज़िन्दा *adj.* alive
zukām जुकाम *n.m.* cold (illness)
zyādā ज़्यादा *adj.* too much; too many

English-Hindi Dictionary

A

able (to be able to) *v.aux.* verb stem + saknā सकना
abortion *n.* garabhpāt *m.* गर्भपात
about *adv.* lagbhag लगभग
actor *n.* abhinetā *m.* अभिनेता
actually *adv.* asal meN असल में
addiction *n.* vyasan *m.* व्यसन
address *n.* patā *m.* पता
advice *n.* salāh *f.* सलाह
after (later) *adv.* bād meN बाद में
after *prep.* ke bād के बाद
agency *n.* ejensī *f.* एजेंसी
aggressive *adj.* laṛākā लड़ाका
agree (to) *v.i. & v.t.* sahamat honā सहमत होना
agreement *n.* sahamati *f.* सहमति
ahead *adv.* āge आगे
AIDS *n.* eḍs *f.* एडस
air *n.* havā *f.* हवा
air conditioning *n.* e. sī. *f.* ए. सी.
airline *n.* havāī kampanī *f.* हवाई कम्पनी
air mail *n.* havāī ḍāk *f.* हवाई डाक
airplane *n.* havāī jahāz *m.* / vimān *m.* हवाई जहाज़ / विमान
airport *n.* havāī aḍḍā *m.* हवाई अड्डा
alarm clock *n.* alārm ghaṛī *f.* अलार्म घड़ी
alcohol *n.* śarāb *f.* शराब
alive *adj.* jīvit / zindā जीवित / ज़िन्दा

all *adj.* sab सब
allergy *n.* elarjī *f.* एलरजी
allow (to) *v.i. & v.t.* anumati denā अनुमति देना
almost *adv.* lagbhag लगभग
alone *adj.* akelā अकेला
already (until now) *adv.* abhī tak अभी तक
also *adv.* bhī भी
altitude *n.* ūNcāī *f.* ऊँचाई
always *adv.* hameśā हमेशा
amazing *adj.* āścaryajanak आश्चर्यजनक
ambassador *n.* rājdūt *m.* राजदूत
ambulance *n.* aspatāl gāṛī *f.* अस्पताल गाड़ी
among *prep.* meN में
ancient *adj.* prācīn प्राचीन
and *conj.* aur और
angry *adj.* nārāz नाराज़
animal *n.* jānvar *m.* जानवर
ankle *n.* ṭakhnā *m.* टखना
anniversary *n.* jayantī *f.* जयन्ती
another (one more) *adj.* ek aur एक और
another (some other) *adj.* dūsrā दूसरा
answer *n.* javāb *m.* जवाब
answer (to) *v.i. & v.t.* javāb denā जवाब देना
ant *n.* cīNṭī *f.* चींटी
antibiotic *n.* pratijaivik *f.* प्रतिजैविक
antique *n.* purāvastu *f.* पुरावसतु
antiseptic *n.* pūtirodhī *f.* पूतिरोधी
anxiety *n.* cintā *f.* चिन्ता
any *adj.* koī कोई
anyone *pron.* koī bhī *m.f.* कोई भी
anything *pron.* kuch bhī *m.f.* कुछ भी
anytime (whenever) *adv.* jab kabhī जब कभी

anywhere *adv.* kahīN bhī कहीं भी
apology *n.* kṣamā yācanā *f.* क्षमा याचना
apple *n.* seb *m.* सेब
appointment *n.* niyojan *m.* नियोजन
archaeology *n.* purātattva *m.* पुरातत्त्व
architect *n.* vāstukār *m.* वास्तुकार
architecture *n.* vāstukalā *f.* वास्तुकला
argue (to) *v.i. & v.t.* bahas karnā बहस करना
army *n.* senā *f.* सेना
arrest (to) *v.t.* giraftār karnā गिरफ़्तार करना
arrival *n.* āgman *m.* आगमन
arrive (to) *v.i.* pahuNcanā पहुँचना
art *n.* kalā *f.* कला
artificial *n.* naqlī *f.* नक़ली
artist *n.* kalākār *m.* कलाकर
ashtray *n.* rākhdānī *f.* राखदानी
ask (to) *v.t.* pūchnā पूछना
aspirin *n.* aisparin *f.* ऐस्पिरिन
asthmatic *n.* damā rogī *m.* दमा रोगी
atmosphere (environment) *n.* vātāvaraṇ *m.* वातावरण
attack (to) *v.i. & v.t.* hamlā karnā हमला करना
automatic *adj.* svacālit स्वचालित
avenue *n.* mārg *m.* मार्ग
average *adj.* ausat औसत
awful *adj.* bhyānak भयानक

B

baby *n.* śiśu *m.* / baccā *m.* शिशु / बच्चा
baby food *n.* bebī fūd *f.* बेबी फूड
babysitter *n.* bacce ko dekhne vālā *m.* / vālī *f.* बच्चे को देखने वाला / वाली

back (of body) *n.* pīṭh *f.* पीठ
backache *n.* pīṭh kā dard *m.* पीठ का दर्द
bad *adj.* burā / qharāb बुरा / ख़राब
bag *n.* tailā *m.* थैला
baggage *n.* sāmān *m.* सामान
balanced *adj.* santulit संतुलित
balcony *n.* chajjā *m.* छज्जा
ball *n.* golā *m.* गोला
bandage *n.* paṭṭī *f.* पट्टी
bank *n.* baiNk *f.* बैंक
bar (cafe) *n.* bār *f.* बार
basil *n.* tulsī *f.* तुलसी
basket *n.* ḍaliyā *f.* डलिया
bath *n.* snān *m.* स्नान
bathe (to bathe oneself) *v.t.* snān karnā / nahānā स्नान करना / नहाना
bathing suit *n.* tairne vāle kapṛe *m.* तैरने वाले कपड़े
bathroom *n.* gusalqhānā *m.* गुसलख़ाना
battery *n.* baiṭrī *f.* बैटरी
be (to) *v.i.* honā होना
beach (seashore) *n.* samudr taṭ *m.* समुद्र तट
beard *n.* dāṛhī *f.* दाढ़ी
beautiful *adj.* sundar सुंदर
because *conj.* kyoNki क्योंकि
become (to) *v.i.* ho jānā हो जाना
bed *n.* bistar *m.* बिस्तर
bedroom *n.* sone kā kamrā *m.* सोने का कमरा
beef *n.* gomāNs *m.* गोमाँस
beer *n.* biyar *f.* बियर
before (earlier) *adv.* pahale पहले
beggar *n.* bhikhārī *f.* भिखारी

begin (to) *v.i. & v.t.* śurū karnā शुरू करना
beginning *n.* śurūāt *f.* शुरूआत
behind *adv.* pīche पीछे
belief *n.* viśvās *m.* विश्वास
believe (to) *v.i.* viśvās karnā विश्वास करना
below *adv.* nīce नीचे
the best *adj.* sabse acchā सबसे अच्छा
between *prep.* bīc meN बीच में
beware! *interj.* qhbardār! ख़बरदार
bicycle *n.* sāikil *f.* साइकिल
big *adj.* baṛā बड़ा
binoculars *n.* dūrbīn *f.* दूरबीन
biography *n.* jīvanī *f.* जीवनी
bird *n.* ciṛiyā *f.* चिड़िया
birth certificate *n.* janmpatr *m.* जन्मपत्र
birthday *n.* janmdin *m.* जन्मदिन
birthplace *n.* janmsthān *m.* जन्मस्थान
bitter *adj.* kaṭu कटु
black *adj.* kālā काला
blanket *n.* kambal *m.* कंबल
bleed (to) *v.i.* qhūn nikalnā खून निकलना
blessing *n.* āśīrvād *m.* आशीर्वाद
blind *adj.* andhā अंधा
bliss *n.* ānand *m.* आनंद
blister *n.* phapholā *m.* फफोला
blood *n.* qhūn *m.* खून
blood pressure *n.* raktacāp *m.* रक्तचाप
blood test *n.* qhūn kī jāNc *f.* खून की जाँच
blouse *n.* kurtī *f.* कुरती
blue *adj.* nīlā नीला
boat *n.* nāv *f.* नाव

body *n.* śrīr *m.* शरीर
bone *n.* haḍḍī *f.* हड्डी
book *n.* kitāb *f.* / pustak *f.* किताब / पुस्तक
bookstore *n.* kitāb kī dukān *f.* किताब की दुकान
boots *n.* būṭ *m.* बूट
border *n.* sīmā *f.* सीमा
bored *adj.* ūbā huā *m.* / huī *f.* ऊबा हुआ / हुई
borrow (to) *v.t.* udhār lenā उधार लेना
botanical *adj.* vānaspatik वानस्पतिक
both *adj.* donoN दोनों
bottle *n.* boṭal *m.* बोटल
bottle opener *n.* boṭal kholne vālā *m.* बोटल खोल्ने वाला
bottom *adj.* nicalā निचला
box *n.* baksā *m.* / sandūk *m.* बक्सा / सन्दूक
boy *n.* laṛkā *m.* लड़का
boyfriend (romantic) *n.* premī *m.* प्रेमी
bracelet *n.* kangan *m.* कंगन
brain *n.* dimāg *m.* दिमाग़
branch (of business) *n.* śākhā *f.* शाखा
brave *adj.* bahādur बहादुर
bread *n.* roṭī *f.* रोटी
break (to) *v.i. & v.t.* ṭūṭnā टूटना
breakfast *n.* nāśtā *m.* नाश्ता
bribe *n.* ghūs *f.* घूस
bride *n.* dulhan *f.* दुल्हन
bridge *n.* pūl *m.* पूल
bring (to) *v.t.* lānā लाना
broom *n.* jhāṛū *m.* झाड़ू
brother *n.* bhāī *m.* भाई
bruise *n.* coṭ *f.* चोट

bucket *n.* bāltī *f.* बाल्टी
Buddha *n.* Buddha *m.* बुध
Buddhist *adj. & n.* bauddhda *m.f.* बौद्ध
bug *n.* kīṛā *m.* कीड़ा
build (to) *v.t.* banānā बनाना
building *n.* imārat *f.* इमारत
burn (to) *v.i.* jalnā जलना
bus *n.* bas *f.* बस
business *n.* vyāpār *m.* व्यापार
bus station *n.* bas kā aḍḍā *m.* बस का अड्डा
bus stop *n.* bas sṭāp *f.* बस स्टाप
busy *adj.* vyast व्यस्त
but *conj.* lekin / magar लेकिन / मगर
butter *n.* makkhan *m.* मक्खन
buy (to) *v.t.* kharīdnā खरीदना

C

calendar *n.* panchāng *m.* पंचांग
calf *n.* bachaṛā *m.* / bachaṛī *f.* बछड़ा / बछड़ी
call (to summon) *v.i. & v.t.* bulānā बुलाना
call (to telephone) *v.t.* fon karnā फ़ोन करना
camera *n.* kaimarā *m.* कैमरा
can (to be able to) *v.aux.* verb stem + saknā सकना
cancel (to) *v.t.* radd karnā रद्द करना
cancellation *n.* mansūkhī *f.* मनसूखी
candle *n.* mombattī *f.* मोमबत्ती
can opener *n.* ṭin kholne vālā *m.* टिन खोलने वाला
capital *n.* rājdhānī *f.* राजधानी
car *n.* gāṛī *m.* गाड़ी

card *n.* kārḍ *m.* कार्ड
care (to take interest) *v.i. & v.t.* parvāh karnā परवा करना
be careful! (*lit.* "go safely!") *interj.* sāvdhānī se jāiye! सावधानी से जाइये
carpet *n.* darī *f.* दरी
carrot *n.* gājar *m.* गाजर
carry (to) *v.i. & v.t.* ḍhonā ढोना
carton *n.* ḍabbā *m.* डब्बा
cash *n.* paisā *m.* पैसा
cashier *n.* qhzāncī *f.* ख़ज़ाानची
cassette *n.* ṭep *m.* टेप
caste *n.* jāti *f.* जाति
cat *n.* billī *f.* बिल्ली
caution *n.* sāvdhānī *f.* सावधानी
cave *n.* gufā *f.* गुफ़ा
celebrate (to) *v.i. & v.t.* manānā मनाना
celebration *n.* samāroh *m.* समारोह
center *n.* kendra *m.* केंद्र
certificate *n.* pramāṇ-patr *m.* प्रमाण-पत्र
chair *n.* kursī *f.* कुर्सी
chance (coincidence) *n.* sanyog *m.* संयोग
change (to) *v.i. & v.t.* badalnā बदलना
change (coins) *n.* ṭūṭe paise *m.* टूटे पैसे
charming *adj.* manohar मनोहर
check *n.* cek *m.* चेक
cheese *n.* panīr *m.* पनीर
chess *n.* śataranj *m.* शतरंज
chessboard *n.* śataranj kī bisāt *f.* शतंरज की बिसात
chest *n.* chātī *f.* छाती
chicken *n.* murgī *f.* मुर्गी

chickpea *n.* chanā *m.* चना
chief *adj.* mukhya मुख्य
child *n.* baccā *m.* / baccī *f.* बच्चा / बच्ची
children *n.* bacce *m.* बच्चे
chili pepper *n.* mirc *f.* मिर्च
Chinese *adj.* cīnī चीनी
chocolate *n.* cākleṭ *f.* चाकलेट
choose (to) *v.t.* cunnā चुनना
Christian *adj. & n.* īsāī *m.* ईसाई
church *n.* girjāghar *m.* गिरजाघर
cigarette *n.* sigreṭ *f.* सिगरेट
cinema *n.* sinemā *m.* सिनेमा
circus *n.* sarkas *m.* सरकस
citizen *n.* nāgrik *m.* नागरिक
citizenship *n.* nāgariktā *f.* नागरिकता
city *n.* śahar *m.* शहर
class (school) *n.* kakṣa *f.* कक्षा
class (social) *n.* varg *m.* वर्ग
clean *adj.* sāf साफ़
cleaning *n.* safāī *f.* सफ़ाई
clear *adj.* spaṣṭ स्पष्ट
climate *n.* jalvāyu *m.* जलवायु
clock *n.* ghaṛī *f.* घड़ी
close (to) *v.t.* band karnā बन्द करना
cloth *n.* kapṛa *m.* कपड़ा
clothing *n.* kapṛe *m.* कपड़े
cloud *n.* bādal *m.* बादल
cockroach *n.* tilcaṭṭā *m.* तिलचट्टा
coffee *n.* kāufī *f.* कौफ़ी
coincidence *n.* sanyog *m.* संयोग
cold *adj.* ṭhaṇḍā ठण्डा

cold (illness) *n.* zukām *m.* जुकाम
college *n.* kālej *m.* कालेज
color *n.* rang *m.* रंग
comb *n.* kanghī *f.* कंघी
come (to) *v.i.* ānā आना
comfortable *adj.* ārāmdāyak आरामदायक
communist *adj. & n.* sāmyavādī *m.* साम्यवादी
community *n.* samudāy *m.* समुदाय
companion *n.* sāthī *m.* साथी
company *n.* kampanī *f.* कंपनी
compare (to) *v.t.* tulnā karnā तुलना करना
complaint *n.* śikāyat *f.* शिकायत
computer *n.* kampyūṭar *f.* कंप्यूटर
conceited *adj.* abhimānī अभिमानी
concert *n.* sangīt samāroh *m.* संगीत समारोह
condom *n.* koṇḍom *m.* कोण्डोम
confidence *n.* viśvās *m.* विश्वास
confirm (to) *v.t.* pakkā karnā पक्का करना
confused *adj.* gaṛbaṛ गड़बड
congratulations! *interj.* badhāī ho! बधाई हो
connection (relation) *n.* sambandh *m.* संबंध
constipation *n.* qabz *f.* क़ब्ज़
constitution (of a state) *n.* sanvidhān *m.* संविधान
construction *n.* nirmāṇ *m.* निर्माण
consulate *n.* dūtāvās *m.* दूतावास
continue (to) *v.i.* caltā rhenā चलता रहना
contraceptive *n.* nirodhak *m.* निरोधक
contract *n.* anubandh *m.* अनुबंध
conversation *n.* bātcīt *f.* बातचीत
cook (a) *n.* qhānsāmā *m.* ख़ानसामा
cook (to) *v.t.* pakānā पकाना

corner *n.* konā *m.* कोना
corpse *n.* lāś *f.* लाश
correct *adj.* ṭhīk ठीक
corruption *n.* bhraṣṭācār *m.* भ्रष्टाचार
cosmic *adj.* antarikṣī अंतरिक्षी
cotton *n.* sūtī *m.* सूती
country *n.* deś *m.* देश
countryside *n.* dehāt *m.* देहात
cough (a) *n.* khāNsī *f.* खाँसी
count (to) *v.t.* ginnā गिनना
court (legal) *n.* adālat *f.* अदालत
cow *n.* gāy (more like gāi) *f.* गाय
crazy *adj.* pāgal पागल
cream *n.* malāī *f.* मलाई
credit *n.* kreḍit *f.* क्रेडित
criminal *n.* aprādhī *m.* अप्राधी
crowd *n.* bhīṛ *f.* भीड़
cucumber *n.* khīrā *m.* खीरा
cup *n.* pyālā *m.* प्याला
cure *n.* rogmukti *f.* रोगमुक्ति
custom (traditions) *n.* rivāz *m.* रिवाज़
customer *n.* grāhak *m.* ग्राहक
cut (a wound) *n.* ghāv *m.* घाव
cut (to) *v.t.* kāṭanā काटना
cycle (to) *v.i.* sāikil calānā साइकिल चलाना

D

dad (father) *n.* pitā-jī *m.* पिता-जी
daily *adj.* rozānā / dainik रोज़ाना / दैनिक
damage *n.* kṣati *f.* क्षति

dance *v.i.* nācnā नाचना
danger *n.* qhatarā *m.* ख़तरा
dangerous *adj.* qhatarnāk ख़तरनाक
dark *adj.* aNdherā अँधेरा
darkness *n.* aNdherā *m.* अँधेरा
date (calendar day) *n.* tārīqh *f.* तारीख़
daughter *n.* beṭī *f.* बेटी
dawn *n.* uṣā-kāl *m.* उषा-काल
day *n.* din *m.* दिन
dead *adj.* marā huā / murdā मरा हुआ / मुरदा
deaf *adj.* baharā बहरा
death *n.* mrityu *f.* मृत्यु
debt *n.* karz *m.* कर्ज़
decide (to) *v.t.* niścay karnā निश्चय
decision *n.* faislā *m.* फ़ैसला
deer *n.* hiran *f.* हिरन
degree (college) *n.* upādhi *f.* उपाधि
delay *n.* der *f.* देर
delicate *adj.* komal कोमल
delicious *adj.* svādiṣṭ स्वादिष्ट
democracy *n.* loktantra *m.* लोकतंत्र
dentist *n.* dantcikitsak *m.* दन्तचिकित्सक
deodorant *n.* ḍiyoḍoraiNṭ *f.* डियोडोरैंट
depart (to) *v.i.* ravānā honā रवाना होना
department *n.* vibhāg *m.* विभाग
departure *n.* prasthān *m.* प्रस्थान
desert *n.* registān *m.* रेगिस्तान
destination *n.* manzil *f.* मंज़िल
destiny *n.* niyati *f.* नियति
diabetes *n.* madhumeha *m.* मधुमेह
diabetic *adj.* madhumehī मधुमेही

diamond *n.* hīrā *m.* हीरा
diaper *n.* potaṛā kaloṭ *m.* पोतड़ा कलोट
diarrhea *n.* dast *m.* दस्त
diary *n.* ḍāyarī *f.* डायरी
dictionary *n.* śabdakoś *m.* शब्दखोश
die (to) *v.i.* marnā मरना
different *adj.* alag अलग
difficult *adj.* muśkil मुश्किल
dinner *n.* rāt kā khānā *m.* रात का खाना
diplomat *n.* rājnayik *m.* राजनयिक
direction *n.* diśā *f.* दिशा
directory *n.* nideśikā *f.* निदेशिका
dirt (soil) *n.* dhūl *f.* धूल
dirty *adj.* gandā गंदा
disabled *adj.* viklāng विकलांग
disadvantage *n.* asuvidhā *f.* असुविधा
disappointment *n.* nirāśā *f.* निराशा
discover (to find out) *v.i.* patā lagānā पता लगाना
discover (to) *v.t.* khoj karnā खोज करना
discrimination *n.* bhed-bhāv *m.* भेद-भाव
discuss (to) *v.t.* … par vicār karnā
… पर विचार करना
discussion *n.* vicār-vimarś *m.* विचार-विमर्श
disease *n.* rog *m.* रोग
disgusting *adj.* ghriṇā yogya घृणा योग्य
dishonest *adj.* beīmān बेईमान
disorder *n.* gaṛbaṛ *f.* गड़बड़
disturb (to agitate) *v.t.* āndolit karnā
अंदोलित करना
disturbance *n.* aśānti *f.* अशान्ति
divorce *n.* talāq *f.* तलाक़

dizziness *n.* cakkar *m.* चक्कर
do (to) *v.t.* karnā करना
doctor *n.* ḍākṭar *m.f.* डॉक्टर
documentation *n.* pralekhan *m.* प्रलेखन
dog *n.* kuttā *m.* कुत्ता
door *n.* darvāzā *m.* दरवाज़ा
down *adv.* nīce नीचे
dozen (a) *n.* darjan *m.* दर्जन
drama (a play) *n.* nāṭak *m.* नाटक
dream (to) *v.i. & v.t.* sapnā dekhnā सपना देखना
drink (to) *v.i.* pīnā पीना
drive (to drive a vehicle) *v.t.* calānā चलाना
drugs (medicine) *n.* davāī *f.* दवाई
drum *n.* ḍhol *m.* ढोल
drunk (to be) *v.i.* naśā caṛhanā नशा चढ़ना
drunkenness *n.* naśā *m.* नशा
dry (to) *v.i. & v.t.* sūkhnā सूखना
during (while) *prep.* … ke daurān … के दौरान
duty *n.* farz *m.* फ़र्ज़
dye *n.* rang *m.* रंग

E

each *adj.* har ek हर एक
ear *n.* kān *m.* कान
early *adv.* jaldī जल्दी
earn (to) *v.t.* kamānā कमाना
earrings *n.* bāliyāN *f.* बालियाँ
Earth *n.* dhartī *f.* धरती
earthquake *n.* bhūkamp *m.* भूकंप
East *n.* pūrva *m.* पूर्व

easy *adj.* āsān आसान
eat (to) *v.i. & v.t.* khānā खाना
economy *n.* arthvyavasthā *f.* अर्थव्यवस्था
editor *n.* sampādak *m.* संपादक
education *n.* śikṣā *f.* शिक्षा
egg *n.* aṇḍā *m.* अण्डा
eggplant *n.* baiNgan *m.* बैंगन
election *n.* cunāv *m.* चुनाव
electricity *n.* bijalī *f.* बिजली
elephant *n.* hāthī *m.* हाथी
embarrassed (to be) *v.i.* śarmindā honā शरमिंदा होना
embassy *n.* dūtāvās *m.* दूतावास
emergency *n.* sankaṭ *m.* संकट
employee *n.* karamcārī *m.f.* कर्मचारी
empty *adj.* qhālī ख़ाली
end *n.* ant *m.* अंत
endure (to) *v.i.* sahanā सहना
engagement *n.* sagāī *f.* सगाई
engine *n.* injan *m.* इंजन
English *n.* aNgrezī *f.* अंग्रेज़ी
enough (adequate) *adj.* kāfī काफ़ी
enough! (stop!) *interj.* bas! बस
enter (to) *v.i. & v.t.* praveś karnā प्रवेश करना
entertainment *n.* manoranjan *m.* मनोरंजन
entrance *n.* praveś *m.* प्रवेश
envelope *n.* lifāfā *m.* लिफ़ाफ़ा
environment *n.* vātāvaraṇ *m.* वातावरण
epileptic *n.* mirgī kā rogī *m.* मिरगी का रोगी
equality *n.* barābarī *f.* बराबरी
especially *adv.* qhās taur se ख़ास तौर से

establish (to) *v.t.* sthāpit karnā स्थापित करना
evening *n.* śām *f.* शाम
everything *pron.* sab kuch *m.f.* सब कुछ
everywhere *adv.* sab jagah सब जगह
examination (school) *n.* parīkṣā *f.* परीक्षा
example *n.* udāharaṇ *m.* उदाहरण
excellent *adj.* baṛhiyā बढ़िया
exchange (money) *n.* vinimay *m.* विनिमय
excuse me! (*lit.* "forgive me!") *interj.* māf kījiye! माफ़ कीजिये
exercise *n.* kasarat *f.* कसरत
exit *n.* nikās *m.* निकास
expensive *adj.* mahaNgā महँगा
explain (to) *v.t.* spaṣṭ karnā स्पष्ट करना
eye *n.* āNkh *f.* आँख
eyeglasses *n.* caśmā *m.* चश्मा

F

face *n.* muNh *m.* मुँह
factory *n.* faikṭarī *f.* फ़ैकटरी
faint (to) *v.i.* behoś ho jānā बेहोश हो जाना
fall (autumn) *n.* śarat *f.* शरत
family *n.* parivār *m.* परिवार
famous *adj.* prasiddh प्रसिद्ध
fan *n.* pankhā *m.* पंखा
far *adj.* dūr दूर
farm *n.* khet *m.* खेत
farmer *n.* kisān *m.* किसान
fast *adj.* tez तेज़
fat *adj.* moṭā मोटा

father *n.* pitā-jī *m.* पिता-जी
fault (guilt) *n.* qgaltī *f.* ग़लती
favorite *adj.* manpasand मनपसंद
fear *n.* ḍar *m.* डर
fear (to be afraid) *v.i.* ḍarnā डरना
feel (to experience) *v.i. & v.t.* mahasūs karnā महसूस करना
fence *n.* bāṛ *m.* बाड़
festival *n.* utsav *m.* उत्सव
fever *n.* buqhār *m.* बुख़ार
few (some) *adj.* kuch कुछ
fiancé / fiancée *n.* maNgetar *m.f.* मँगेतर
field (agricultural) *n.* khet *m.* खेत
fight *n.* laṛāī *f.* लड़ाई
film *n.* film *f.* फ़िल्म
find (to) *v.t.* pānā पाना
find (to find out) *v.t.* patā lagānā पता लगाना
finger *n.* aNgulī *f.* अँगुली
fire *n.* āg *f.* आग
first *n.* pahalā *m.* पहला
fish *n.* machlī *f.* मछली
flag *n.* jhaṇḍā *m.* झण्डा
flashlight *n.* ṭārc *m.* टॉर्च
flat *adj.* samatal समतल
flea *n.* pissū *m.* पिस्सू
flight *n.* uṛān *f.* उड़ान
floor *n.* farś *m.* फ़र्श
flour *n.* āṭā *m.* आटा
flower *n.* phūl *m.* फूल
fly *n.* makkhī *f.* मक्खी
fly (to) *v.i.* uṛnā उड़ना

fog *n.* kuharā *m.* कुहरा
follow (to) *v.i. & v.t.* pīche-pīche calnā पीछे-पीछे चलना
food *n.* khānā *m.* खाना
foot *n.* pair *m.* पैर
foreign *adj.* videśī विदेशी
foreigner *n.* videśī *m.* विदेशी
forest *n.* van *m.* वन
forever *adv.* sadā ke liye सदा के लिये
forget (to) *v.i.* bhūl jānā भूल जाना
forgive (to) *v.t.* kṣamā karnā / māf karnā क्षमा करना / माफ़ करना
fragile *adj.* bhangur / nāzuk भंगुर / नाज़ुक
free (no charge) *adj.* muft मुफ़्त
freedom *n.* svtantratā *f.* स्वतंत्रता
fresh *adj.* tāzā ताज़ा
fried *adj.* talā huā तला हुआ
fruit *n.* phal *m.* फल
fry (to) *v.t.* talnā तलना
fuel (gas) *n.* peṭrol *m.* पेट्रोल
full *adj.* pūrṇ पूर्ण
fun *adj.* mazā मज़ा
fun (to have) *v.i.* mazā ānā मज़ा आना
funeral (Hindu cremation rite) *n.* dāh sanskār *m.* दाह संस्कार
future *n.* bhaviṣya *m.* भविष्य

G

game *n.* khel *m.* खेल
garbage *n.* raddī *f.* रद्दी

garden *n.* bāqg *m.* बाग़
garlic *n.* lehsun *m.* लहसुन
gay (homosexual) *adj.* qhuś खुश
generosity *n.* udārtā *f.* उदारता
genuine (pure) *adj.* śuddh शुद्ध
get (to) *v.t.* pānā पाना
gift (present) *n.* upahār *m.* उपहार
girl *n.* laṛkī *f.* लड़की
girlfriend (romantic) *n.* premikā *f.* प्रेमिका
give (to) *v.t.* denā देना
glass *n.* śīśā *m.* शीशा
glasses (eye) *n.* caśmā *m.* चश्मा
go (to) *v.i.* jānā जाना
goal *n.* lakṣay *m.* लक्ष्य
goat *n.* bakarā *m.* बकरा
God *n.* allāh *m.* (Muslim) / bhagavān *m.* (Hindu) अल्लाह / भगवान
gold *n.* sonā *m.* सोना
good *adj.* acchā अच्छा
good-bye! *interj.* namaste! *inf.* /namaskār! *for.* नमस्ते / नमस्कार
good night! *interj.* śubh rātri! शुभ रात्रि
government *n.* sarkār *f.* सरकार
grammar *n.* vyākaraṇ *m.* व्याकरण
grandfather (maternal) *n.* nānā *m.* नाना
grandfather (paternal) *n.* dādā *m.* दादा
grandmother (maternal) *n.* nānī *f.* नानी
grandmother (paternal) *n.* dādī *f.* दादी
grape *n.* angūr *m.* अंगूर
grass *n.* ghās *f.* घास
green *adj.* harā हरा

group *n.* samūh *m.* समूह
guarantee *n.* gāranṭī *f.* गॉरंटी
guest *n.* atithi / mehamān *m.f.* अतिथि / मेहमान
guilt *n.* doṣ *m.* दोष
gun *n.* bandūk *f.* बन्दूक
gynecologist (*lit.* "women's doctor") *n.*
auratoN kā ḍākṭar *m.* / auratoN kī ḍākṭar *f.*
औरतों का डाकटर / औरतों की डाकटर

H

habit *n.* ādat *f.* आदत
hair (of body) *n.* rom *m.* रोम
hair (of head) *n.* bāl *m.* बाल
hairbrush *n.* bāloN kā braś *m.* बालों का ब्रश
haircut *n.* bāl kaṭāī *m.* बाल कटाई
half *n.* ādhā *m.* आधा
hallucination *n.* matibhram *m.* मतिभ्रम
hammer *n.* hathauṛā *m.* हथौड़ा
hand *n.* hāth *m.* हाथ
handbag *n.* haiNḍ baig *m.* हैंड बैग
handicapped *adj.* viklāng विकलांग
handkerchief *n.* rumāl *m.* रुमाल
handmade *adj.* hāth kā banā हाथ का बना
handsome *adj.* manohār मनोहार
hang (to hang on wall, etc.) *v.t.* ṭāNgnā टाँगना
happen (to) *v.i.* ho jānā हो जाना
happiness *n.* qhuśī *m.* ख़ुशी
happy *adj.* qhuś ख़ुश
harassment *n.* pareśānī *f.* परेशानी
hard *adj.* kaṛā कड़ा

hashish *n.* bhāNg *f.* भाँग
hat *n.* ṭopī *f.* टोपी
hatred *n.* nafrat *f.* नफ़रत
he *pron.* voh (at a distance) *m.* / yeh (nearby) *m.*
वह / यह
head *n.* sir *m.* सिर
headache *n.* sardard *m.* सिरदर्द
health *n.* tabīyat *f.* तबीयत
hear (to) *v.i. & v.t.* sunnā सुनना
heart *n.* dil *m.* दिल
heat *n.* garmī *f.* गरमी
heater *n.* hīṭar *m.* हीटर
heavy *adj.* bhārī भारी
height *n.* ūNcāī *f.* ऊँचाई
hello! *interj.* namaste! *inf.* / namaskār! *for.*
नमस्ते / नमस्कार
help! *interj.* bacāo! बचाओ
help *n.* madad *f.* मदद
help (to) *v.t.* madad karnā मदद करना
herbs *n.* jaṛī-būṭī *f.* जड़ी-बूटी
here *adv.* yahāN यहाँ
hiccup *n.* hicakī *f.* हिचकी
high *adj.* ūNcā ऊँचा
hike *v.t.* paidal sair karnā पैदल सैर करना
hill *n.* pahāṛī *f.* पहाड़ी
Hindu *adj. & n.* hindū *m.f.* हिन्दू
historical *adj.* aitihāsik ऐतिहासिक
history *n.* itihās *m.* इतिहास
hit (to) *v.t.* mārnā मारना
holiday (celebrated day) *n.* tyohār *m.* त्योहार
holiday (vacation) *n.* chuṭṭī *f.* छुट्टी

holy *adj.* pavitr पवित्र
home *n.* ghar *m.* घर
homeless *adj.* beghar बेघर
homosexual *adj.* samlingkāmī समलिंगकामी
homosexuality *n.* samlingkāmuktā *f.* समलिंगकामुकता
honey *n.* madhu *m.* मधु
honor *n.* sammān *m.* सम्मान
hope *n.* āśā *f.* आशा
horse *n.* ghoṛā *m.* घोड़ा
hospital *n.* aspatāl *m.* अस्पताल
hot *adj.* garam गरम
how *adv.* kaise कैसे
human *n.* mānav *m.* मानव
human rights *n.* mānav adhikār *m.* मानव अधिकार
humidity *n.* umas *m.* उमस
hunger *n.* bhūk *f.* भूक
hungry *adj.* bhūkhā भूखा
husband *n.* pati *m.* पति

I

I *pron.* maiN *m.f.* मैं
ice *n.* barf *f.* बर्फ़
ice cream *n.* āiskrīm *f.* आइसक्रीम
identification *n.* pahicān *f.* पहिचान
idiotic *adj.* mūrkh मुर्ख
if *conj.* yadi / agar यदि / अगर
ill *adj.* bīmār बीमार
illness *n.* bīmārī *f.* बीमारी
imagine (to) *v.t.* kalpnā karnā कल्पना करना

immigrant *adj. & n.* āpravāsī *m.* आप्रवासी
immigration *n.* āpravās *m.* आप्रवास
immunization *n.* pratirakṣīkaraṇ *m.* प्रतिरक्षीकरण
impatient *adj.* becain बेचैन
important *adj.* mahatvapūrṇ महत्त्वपूर्ण
impossible *adj.* asambhav असंभव
improper (wrong) *adj.* aśuddh अशद्ध
incense *n.* dhūp *m.* धूप
include (to) *v.t.* śāmil karnā शामिल करना
inconceivable *adj.* abhāvanīy अभावनीय
incredible *adj.* aviśvasnīy अविश्वसनीय
independence *n.* svatantratā *f.* स्वतंत्रता
independent *adj.* svatantra स्वतंत्र
indigestion *n.* badhazamī *f.* बदहज़मी
industry *n.* udyog *m.* उद्योग
inequality *n.* asamāntā *f.* असमानता
infection *n.* sandūṣaṇ *m.* संदूषण
inflammation *n.* sūjan *f.* सूजन
injection *n.* sūī *f.* सूई
injury *n.* coṭ *f.* चोट
insane *adj.* pāgal पागल
inside *adv.* andar अन्दर
inside *prep.* meN में
in spite of *prep.* … ke bāvjūd … के बावजूद
institute *n.* sansthān *m.* संस्थान
insurance *n.* bīmā *m.* बीमा
intelligent *adj.* buddhimān बुद्धिमान
interesting *adj.* dilcasp दिल्चस्प
international *adj.* antarrāṣṭrīy अंतरराष्ट्रीय
international call *n.* antarrāṣṭrīy fon *m.* अंतरराष्ट्रीय फ़ोन

interpreter *n.* dubhāṣiyā *m.* दुभाषिया
intersection (of roads) *n.* caurāhā *m.* चौराहा
intestines *n.* aNtaṛī *f.* अँतड़ी
intoxication (from life) *n.* mastī *f.* मस्ती
intoxication (from substance) *n.* naśā *m.* नशा
introduce (to) *v.t.* paricay denā परिचय देना
introduction *n.* paricay *m.* परिचय
invitation *n.* nimantraṇ *m.* निमंत्रण
iron (to press) *v.t.* istrī karnā इस्तरी करना
island *n.* ṭāpū *m.* टापू
itch *n.* khujlī *f.* खुजली
itinerary *n.* yātrākram *m.* यात्राक्रम

J

jacket *n.* jākeṭ *f.* जाकेट
jail *n.* jel *m.* जेल
jar *n.* martabān *m.* मर्तबान
jasmine *n.* camelī *f.* चमेली
jaw *n.* jabaṛā *m.* जबड़ा
jealous *adj.* īrṣyālu ईर्ष्यालु
jealousy *n.* jalan *f.* जलन
jewel *n.* maṇi *f.* मणि
jewelry *n.* javāharāt *m.* जवाहरात
Jewish *adj.* yahūdī यहूदी
job *n.* naukrī *f.* नौकरी
joke *n.* mazāk *m.* मज़ाक
joke (to) *v.t.* mazāk karnā मज़ाक करना
journalist *n.* patrakār *m.* पत्रकार
journey *n.* yātrā *f.* यात्रा
judge *n.* jaj *m.* जज

juice *n.* ras *m.* रस
jump (to) *v.i.* kūdnā कूदना
just (only) *adv.* keval / sirf केवल / सिर्फ़
justice *n.* nyāy *m.* न्याय

K

keep (to) *v.i. & v.t.* rakhnā रखना
key *n.* cābī *f.* चाबी
kick (to) *v.t.* ṭhokar mārnā ठोकर मारना
kidney *n.* gurdā *m.* गुर्दा
kill (to) *v.t.* mār ḍālnā मार डालना
kilogram *n.* kilogrām *m.* किलोग्राम
kilometer *n.* kilomīṭar *m.* किलोमीटर
kind *adj.* kripālu कृपालु
king *n.* rājā *m.* राजा
kiss *n.* cummā *m.* चुम्मा
kiss (to) *v.t.* cūmnā चूमना
kitchen *n.* rasoīghar *m.* रसोईघर
kitten *n.* bilauṭā *m.* बिलैटा
knee *n.* ghuṭnā *m.* घुटना
knife *n.* cāqū *m.* चाक़ू
knock (to) *v.t.* khaṭkhṭānā खटखटाना
know (to know / recognize someone) *v.t.* pahacānnā पहचानना
know (to know something) *v.t.* jānnā जानना

L

lace (string) *n.* fītā *m.* फ़ीता
ladder *n.* sīṛhī *f.* सीढ़ी

lady (woman) *n.* aurat *f.* औरत
lake *n.* jhīl *f.* झील
land (soil) *n.* bhūmi *f.* भूमि
landscape *n.* bhū-draśy *m.* भू-दृश्य
language *n.* bhāṣā *f.* भाषा
lantern *n.* lālṭen *f.* लालटेन
large *adj.* baṛā बड़ा
last (final) *adj.* āntim अन्तिम
last (previous) *adj.* pichlā पिछला
late *adv.* der देर
laugh (to) *v.i.* haNsnā हँसना
laughter *n.* haNsī *f.* हँसी
laundry *n.* dhobīqhānā *m.* धोबीख़ाना
law *n.* qānūn *m.* क़ानून
lawyer *n.* vakīl *m.* वकील
laxative *n.* dastāvar *m.* दस्तावर
lazy *adj.* ālsī आलसी
leader *n.* netā *m.* नेता
leaf *n.* pattā *m.* पत्ता
learn (to) *v.t.* sīkhnā सीखना
leather *n.* camṛā *m.* चमड़ा
ledge *n.* kagār *f.* कगार
left *adj.* bāyāN बायाँ
leg *n.* ṭāNg *m.* टाँग
legal *adj.* qānūnī क़ानूनी
legalization *n.* vaidhīkaraṇ *m.* वैधीकरण
lemon *n.* nībū *m.* नीबू
lens *n.* lens *m.* लेन्स
lesbian *adj. & n.* lezbiyan *f.* / qhuś (gay) *adj.m.f.* लेज़बियन / खुश
less *adj.* kam कम

letter *n.* ciṭṭhī *f.* चिट्ठी
liar *n.* jhūṭhā *m.* झूठा
library *n.* pustakālay *m.* पुस्तकालय
lice *n.* jueN *f.* जुएँ
lie (falsehood) *n.* jhūṭh *m.* झूठ
lie (to) *v.i. & v.t.* jhūṭh bolnā झूठ बोलना
life *n.* jīvan *m.* / zindagī *f.* जीवन / ज़िन्दगी
light *n.* prakāś *m.* प्रकाश
lightbulb *n.* battī *f.* बत्ती
lighter *n.* jalānevālā *m.* जलानेवाला
lightning *n.* bijlī *f.* बिजली
like *adj.* samān समान
like (to) *v.t.* pasand karnā पसंद करना
line (queue) *n.* lāin *f.* लाइन
lion *n.* sinha *m.* / śer *m.* सिंह / शेर
lip *n.* hoNṭh *m.* होंठ
liquor *n.* śarāb *f.* शराब
listen (to) *v.t.* sunnā सुनना
little (small) *adj.* choṭā छोटा
little (a small amount) *adj.* thoṛā थोड़ा
live (to exist) *v.t.* jīnā जीना
live (to live somewhere or stay somewhere) *v.t.* rehenā रहना
loan *n.* udhār *m.* उधार
local *adj.* sthānīy स्थानीय
location (place) *n.* sthān *m.* स्थान
lock *n.* tālā *m.* ताला
lock (to) *v.t.* tālā lagānā ताला लगाना
lonely *adj.* akelā अकेला
long *adj.* lambā लम्बा
look (to) *v.t.* dekhnā देखना

look after (to care for) *v.t.* dekhbhāl karnā देखभाल करना
lose (to) *v.t.* khonā खोना
loss *n.* aprāpti *f.* अप्राप्ति
a lot *adj.* bahut बहुत
loud *adj.* tez तेज़
love *n.* prem *m.* / pyār *m.* / muhabbat *f.* प्रेम / प्यार / मुहब्बत
love (to) *v.t.* pyār karnā प्यार करना
lover *n.* premī *m.* / premikā *f.* प्रेमी / प्रेमिका
low *adv.* nīce नीचे
loyal *adj.* vafādār वफ़ादार
luck *n.* bhāgya *m.* भाग्य
lucky *adj.* saubhāgyaśālī सौभाग्यशाली
luggage *n.* sāmān *m.* सामान
lump *n.* ḍhelā *m.* ढेला
lunch *n.* din kā khānā *m.* दिन का खाना
lungs *n.* phephṛā *m.* फेफड़ा
luxury *n.* aiś *m.* ऐश

M

machine *n.* maśīn *f.* मशीन
mad (angry) *adj.* qgussā गुस्सा
mad (crazy) *adj.* pāgal पागल
magazine (periodical) *n.* patrikā *f.* पत्रिका
magic *n.* jādū *m.* जादू
magician *n.* jādūgar *m.* जादूगर
mail *n.* ḍāk *f.* डाक
majority *n.* bahumat *m.* बहुमत
make (to) *v.t.* banānā बनाना
man *n.* ādmī *m.* आदमी

manager *n.* mainejar *m.* मैनेजर
many (a lot) *adj.* bahut बहुत
map *n.* naqśā *m.* नक़्शा
marijuana *n.* gānjā *f.* गांजा
market *n.* bāzār *m.* बाज़ार
marriage *n.* śādī *f.* शादी
marry (to) *v.t.* śādī karnā शादी करना
massage *n.* māliś *f.* मालिश
mat *n.* caṭāī *f.* चटाई
match(es) *n.* diyāsalāī *f.s.* / mācis *f.pl.* दियासलाई / माचिस
mattress *n.* caṭāī *f.* चटाई
maybe *adv.* śāyad शायद
meal *n.* bhojan *m.* भोजन
meaning *n.* arth *m.* अर्थ
meaningful *adj.* arthpūrṇ अर्थपूर्ण
meat *n.* māNs *m.* मांस
mechanic *n.* maikenik *m.* मैकेनिक
medal *n.* padak *m.* पदक
medicine *n.* davā *f.* दवा
meet (to) *v.i. & v.t.* … se milnā … से मिलना
member *n.* sadasya *m.* सदस्य
memory *n.* yād *f.* याद
menstruation *n.* māhavārī *f.* माहवारी
mental *adj.* mānsik मानसिक
mental illness *n.* mānsik bīmārī *f.* मानसिक बीमारी
menu *n.* menyū *m.* मेन्यू
message *n.* sandeś *m.* सन्देश
metal *n.* dhātu *f.* धातु
meteor *n.* ulkā *f.* उल्का
midnight *n.* madhyarātri *f.* मध्यरात्रि

midwife *n.* dāī *f.* दाई
migraine *n.* ādhāsīsī *f.* आधासीसी
military *n.* senā *f.* सेना
milk *n.* dūdh *m.* दूध
million (a) *n.* das lākh *m.* दस लाख
mind *n.* man *m.* मन
mineral water (*lit.* "bottled water") *n.* botal kā pānī *m.* बोतल का पानी
minute (a) *n.* ek minaṭ *m.* एक मिनट
mirror *n.* darpaṇ *m.* दर्पण
miscarriage *n.* garabhpāt *m.* बर्भपात
miss (to feel the absence of) *v.t.* … kī kamī mehasūs karnā … की कमी महसूस करना
mistake *n.* bhūl *f.* भूल
modesty *n.* sankoc *m.* संकोच
monastery *n.* maṭh *m.* मठ
Monday *n.* somvār *m.* सोमवार
money *n.* paisā *m.* पैसा
monk *n.* tapasvī *m.* तपस्वी
month *n.* mahīnā *m.* महीना
monument *n.* smārak *m.* स्मारक
mood *n.* mijāz *f.* मिजाज़
moon *n.* candra *m.* चन्द्र
more *adj.* zyādā ज़्यादा
morning *n.* saverā *m.* सवेरा
mosque *n.* masjid *f.* मस्जिद
mosquito *n.* macchar *m.* मच्छडर
mother *n.* mātā-jī *f.* माता-जी
motorcycle *n.* moṭar sāikil *f.* मोटर साइकिल
mountain *n.* pahāṛ *m.* पहाड़
mourning *n.* śok *m.* शोक

movie *n.* film *f.* फ़िल्म
mud *n.* kīcaṛ *m.* कीचड़
muscle *n.* mānspeśī *f.* मांसपेशी
museum *n.* sangrahālay *m.* संग्रहालय
music *n.* sangīt *m.* संगीत
musician *n.* sangītkār *m.* संगीतकार
Muslim *adj. & n.* musalmānī मुसलमानी; musalmān *m.* मुसलमान
my *pron.* merā *m.s* /mere *m.pl.* / merī *f.s.pl.* मेरा / मेर / मेरी (object determines gender and number)

N

nail (hardware) *n.* kīl *f.* कील
nail (of person) *n.* nakh *m.* नख
naive *adj.* bholā-bhālā भोला-भाला
naked *adj.* nangā नंगा
name *n.* nām *m.* नाम
nap *n.* jhapak *f.* झपक
napkin *n.* naipkin *f.* नैपकिन
narrow *adj.* tang तंग
nation *n.* rāṣṭra *m.* राष्ट्र
national *adj.* rāṣṭrīy राष्ट्रीय
nationality *n.* rāṣṭrīyatā *f.* राष्ट्रीयता
natural (of behavior, etc.) *adj.* svābhāvik स्वाभाविक
natural (of the Earth, etc.) *adj.* prākritik प्राकृतिक
nature (of the Earth, etc.) *n.* prakriti *f.* प्रकृति
nature (as in human nature) *n.* svabhāv *m.* स्वभाव
nausea *n.* miclī *f.* मिचली

near *adv.* pās पास
necessary *adj.* āvaśyak आवश्यक
necklace *n.* kaṇṭhī *f.* कण्ठी
need (to) *v.t.* cāhanā चाहना
need (I need X) *phr.* mujhe ... cāhiye
मुझे ... चाहिये
neighbor *n.* paṛosī *m.* पड़ोसी
never *adv.* kabhī nahīN कभी नहीं
new *adj.* nayā नया
news *n.* samācār *m.* समाचार
newspaper *n.* samācārpatr *m.* समाचारपत्र
New Year's Day *n.* navvarṣ *m.* नववर्ष
next *adj.* aglā अगला
nice *adj.* acchā अच्छा
night *n.* rāt *f.* रात
no *adv.* nahīN नहीं
nobody *pron.* koī nahīN *m.f.* कोई नहीं
noise *n.* śor *m.* शोर
noisy (it's very) *adj.* bahut śor बहुत शोर
none *pron.* koī bhī nahīN *m.f.* कोई भी नहीं
noon *n.* dopahar *f.* दोपहर
North *adj. & n.* uttar *m.* उत्तर
nose *n.* nāk *f.* नाक
notebook *n.* kāpī *f.* कॉपी
nothing *adv.* kuch nahīN कुछ नहीं
not yet *adv.* ab tak nahīN अब तक नहीं
novel (type of book) *n.* upanyās *m.* उपन्यास
now *adv.* ab अब
nowhere *adv.* kahīN nahīN कहीं नहीं
nuclear energy *n.* parmāṇu ūrjā *f.* परमाणु ऊर्जा
number *n.* sankhyā *m.* संख्या

nun *n.* maṭhvāsinī *f.* मठवासिनी
nurse *n.* nars *f.* नर्स

O

object (to) *v.t.* virodh karnā विरोध करना
obtain (to) *v.t.* pānā पाना
occasionally *adv.* kabhī kabhī कभी कभी
occupation *n.* peśā *m.* पेशा
occupied (busy) *adj.* vyast व्यस्त
ocean *n.* mahāsāgar *m.* महासागर
odd (strange) *adj.* anokhā अनोखा
offensive (insulting) *adj.* apmānjanak अपमानजनक
offer (to raise / lift up) *v.t.* caṛhānā चढ़ाना
offering (religious) *n.* caṛāvā *m.* चढ़ावा
office *n.* daftar *m.* दफ़्तर
often *adv.* aksar अक्सर
oil *n.* tel *m.* तेल
OK! *interj.* ṭhīk hai! ठीक है
old (person) *adj.* būṛhā बूढ़ा
old (thing) *adj.* purānā पुराना
olive(s) *n.* zaitūn *m.* ज़ैतून
on *prep.* … par … पर
once (one occurrence) *adv.* ek bār एक बार
one *adj.* ek एक
onion *n.* pyāz *m.* प्याज़
only *adj.* keval / sirf केवल / सिर्फ़
on time *adj. & adv.* samay par समय पर
open *adj.* khulā खुला
open (to) *v.t.* kholnā खोलना

operation *n.* āpreśn *m.* ऑप्रेशन
opinion *n.* ray (more like rai) *f.* राय
opportunity *n.* avsar *m.* अवसर
opposite *adj.* sāmne kā सामने का
or *conj.* yā या
orange (color) *adj.* nārangī नारंगी
orange (fruit) *n.* santarā *m.* संन्तरा
order (to place an order) *v.i. & v.t.* ārḍr karnā ऑर्डर करना
ordinary *adj.* māmūlī मामूली
organization (structure) *n.* sangaṭhan *m.* संगठन
original *adj.* mūl मूल
other *adj.* dūsrā दूसरा
out *adv.* bāhar बाहर
outside *n.* bāhar *m.* बाहर
owner *n.* mālik *m.* मालिक
over *adv.* ūpar ऊपर
oxygen *n.* āksījan *m.* ऑकसीजन

P

Pacific Ocean *n.* praśānt mahāsāgar *m.* प्रशान्त महासागर
pack *n.* poṭalā *m.* पोटला
package (parcel) *n.* pārsal *m.* पार्सल
padlock *n.* tālā *m.* ताला
page *n.* pannā *m.* पन्ना
pain *n.* dard *m.* दर्द
painful *adj.* dardnāk दर्दनाक
painkiller *n.* dard kī davā *f.* दर्द की दवो
paint (to) *v.i. & v.t.* tasvīr banānā तस्वीर बनाना

painter *n.* citrakār *m.* चित्रकार
palace *n.* rājbhavan *m.* / mahal *m.* राजभवन / महल
pan *n.* tavā *m.* तवा
pants *n.* patlūn *m.* पतलून
paper *n.* kāqgaz *m.* काग़ज़
paradise *n.* svarg *m.* स्वर्ग
parents *n.* mātā-pitā *m.* माता-पिता
park *n.* pārk *m.* पार्क
parliament *n.* sansad *f.* संसद
part *n.* bhāg *m.* / hissā *m.* भाग / हिस्सा
participation *n.* sahyog *m.* सहयोग
party *n.* parṭī *f.* पार्टी
pass (mountain) *n.* ghāṭī *f.* घाटी
passenger *n.* yātrī *m.* / savārī *f.* यात्री / सवारी
passport *n.* pāsporṭ *m.* पासपोर्ट
passport number *n.* pāsport nambar *m.* पासपोर्ट नंबर
past *adj.* bītā huā बीता हुआ
path *n.* path *m.* / rāstā *m.* पथ / रास्ता
patience *n.* dhīraj *m.* धीरज
pay (to) *v.t.* paise denā पैसे देना
payment *n.* bhugtān *m.* भुगतान
peace *n.* śānti *f.* शान्ति
peaceful *adj.* śāntipūrṇ शान्तिपूर्ण
peak (mountain) *n.* coṭī *f.* चोटी
peanut *n.* mūNgfalī *f.* मूँगफ़ली
pen *n.* qalam *f.* क़लम
pencil *n.* pensil *f.* पेंसिल
penis *n.* ling *m.* लिंग
people *n.* log *m.* लोग
pepper (black) *n.* kālī mīrc *f.* काली मिर्च

pepper (red) *n.* lāl mīrc *f.* लाल मिर्च
percent *n.* pratiśat *m.* प्रतिशत
perfume *n.* sugandh *f.* सुगन्ध
perhaps *adv.* śāyad शायद
period (menstrual) pain *n.* māsik kā dard *m.* मासिक का दर्द
permanent *adj.* sthāyī स्थायी
permission *n.* anumati *f.* अनुमति
permit *n.* anumati-patr *m.* अनुमति-पत्र
permit (to) *v.t.* anumati denā अनुमति देना
person *n.* vyakti *m.* व्यक्ति
personality *n.* vyaktitva *m.* व्यक्तित्व
perspire (to) *v.i.* pasīnā nikalnā पसीना निकलना
pharmacy *n.* davā-qhānā *m.* दवा-ख़ाना
phone *n.* fon *m.* फ़ोन
photo *n.* foṭo *m.* फ़ोटो
photography *n.* foṭogrāfī *f.* फ़ोटोग्राफ़ी
piece *n.* ṭukṛā *m.* टुकड़ा
pig *n.* sūar *m.* सूअर
pill *n.* golī *f.* गोली
pillow *n.* takiyā *m.* तकिया
pillowcase *n.* takiye kā gilāf *m.* तकिये का गिलाफ़
pilot *n.* pāylaṭ *m.* पायलट
pineapple *n.* anannās *m.* अनन्नास
pink *adj.* gulābī गुलाबी
pipe *n.* cilam *f.* चिलम
place *n.* sthān *m.* स्थान
place of birth *n.* janam sthān *m.* जन्म स्थान
plain *adj.* sādā सादा
plan *n.* yojnā *f.* योजना
plane (airplane) *n.* vimān *m.* / havāī jahāz *f.* विमान / हवाई जहाज़

planet *n.* grah *m.* ग्रह
plant *n.* paudhā *m.* पौधा
plant (to) *v.t.* bonā बोना
plastic *n.* plāsṭik *f.* प्लास्टिक
plate *n.* pleṭ *f.* / thālī *f.* प्लेट / थाली
platform *n.* pleṭfārm *m.* प्लेटफ़ार्म
play (drama) *n.* nāṭak *m.* नाटक
please *adv.* krpayā कृपया
pleasure (sensual) *n.* vilās *m.* विलास
pocket *n.* jeb *f.* जेब
poetry *n.* kāvya *m.* काव्य
poison *n.* zahar *m.* ज़हर
poisonous *adj.* zahardār ज़हरदार
police *n.* pulis *f.* पुलिस
politician *n.* politiśan *m.* पॉलिटिशण
politics *n.* rājnīti *f.* राजनीति
pollution *n.* pradūṣaṇ *m.* प्रदूषण
poor *adj.* qgarīb ग़रीब
popular *adj.* lokpriya लोकप्रिय
population *n.* janasankhyā *f.* जनसंख्या
possible *adj.* sambhav संभव
postage *n.* mehsūl *m.* महसूल
postal code (zip code) *n.* pin koḍ *m.* पिन कोड
postcard *n.* posṭ-kārḍ *m.* पोस्ट-कार्ड
post office *n.* ḍākghar *m.* डाकघर
pottery *n.* kumhārī *f.* कुम्हारी
poverty *n.* qgarībī *f.* ग़रीबी
power *n.* śakti *f.* शक्ति
pray (to) *v.t.* prārthnā karnā प्रार्थना करना
prayer *n.* prārthnā *f.* प्रार्थना
pregnant *n.* garabhvatī *f.* गर्भवती

prepare (to) *v.t.* taiyār karnā तैयार करना
prescription (medical) *n.* nusqhā *m.* नुसख़ा
present (gift) *n.* upahār *m.* / tohfā *m.* उपहार / तोहफ़ा
presentation *n.* prastutīkaraṇ *f.* प्रस्तुतीकरण
president (of a country) *n.* rāṣṭrapati *m.* राष्ट्रपति
pressure *n.* dāb *f.* दाब
pretty *adj.* sundar सुन्दर
price *n.* dām *m.* दाम
pride *n.* garv *m.* गर्व
priest (Christian) *n.* pādrī *m.* पादरी
priest (Hindu) *n.* pujārī *m.* पुजारी
priest (Muslim) *n.* maulavī *m.* मौलवी
prime minister *n.* pradhān mantrī *m.f.* प्रधान मंत्री
prison *n.* jelqhānā *m.* जेलख़ाना
prisoner *n.* bandī *m.* बन्दी
private (personal) *adj.* vyaktigat व्यक्तिगत
problem *n.* samasyā *f.* समस्या
profession *n.* vyavasāy *m.* / peśā *m.* व्यवसाय / पेशा
profit *n.* lābh *m.* लाभ
program *n.* kārykram *m.* कार्यक्रम
projector *n.* projekṭar *m.* प्रोजेक्टर
promise *n.* vādā *m.* वादा
proposal *n.* prastāv *m.* प्रस्ताव
protect (to) *v.t.* rakṣā karnā रक्षा करना
protest *n.* virodh *m.* विरोध
protest (to) *v.i. & v.t.* virodh karnā विरोध करना
pure *adj.* śuddh शुद्ध
purple *adj.* baiNganī बैंगनी
push (to) *v.t.* dhakelnā धकेलना
put (to) *v.t.* rakhnā रखना

Q

qualifications *n.* yogyatā *f.* योग्यता
quality *n.* guṇ *m.* गुण
quarantine *n.* sangrodh *m.* संगरोध
quarrel *n.* jhagṛā *m.* झगड़ा
queen *n.* rānī *f.* रानी
question *n.* praśn *m.* /savāl *m.* प्रश्न / सवाल
question (to ask a) *v.t.* pūchnā पूछना
quick *adj.* tez तेज़
quickly *adv.* jaldī *f.* जल्दी
quiet *n.* śānt *m.* शान्त
quinine *n.* kunain *f.* कुनैन
quit (to) *v.t.* choṛ denā छोड़ देना

R

rabbit *n.* qhargoś *m.* ख़रगोश
race (of people) *n.* jāti *f.* जाति
racism *n.* jātivād *m.* जातिवाद
radiator *n.* reḍiyeṭar *m.* रेडियेटर
radio *n.* reḍiyo *m.* रेडियो
radio broadcast *n.* prasāraṇ *m.* प्रसारण
radish *n.* mūlī *f.* मूली
railroad *n.* relve *f.* रेलवे
railroad station *n.* relve sṭeśan *m.* रेलवे स्टेशन
rain *n.* bāriś *f.* बारिश
rainbow *n.* indradhnuṣ *m.* इन्द्र्धनुष
raining (it's) *phr.* bāriś ho rahī hai बारिश हो रही है
raisin *n.* kiśmiś *f.* किशमिश
rally *n.* railī *f.* रैली

rape *n.* balātkār *m.* बलात्कार
rare (infrequent) *adj.* viral विरल
rash *n.* dadorā *m.* ददोरा
rat *n.* cūhā *m.* चूहा
raw (uncooked) *adj.* kaccā कच्चा
razor *n.* ustarā *m.* उस्तरा
read (to) *v.i. & v.t.* paṛhnā पढ़ना
ready *adj.* taiyār तैयार
ready (to be) *v.i.* taiyār ho jānā तैयार हो जाना
real *adj.* aslī असली
rear *n.* pichāṛī *f.* पिछाड़ी
reason (cause) *n.* kāraṇ *m.* कारण
receipt *n.* rasīd *f.* रसीद
receive (to) *v.t.* prāpt karnā प्राप्त करना
recent *adj.* hāl kā हाल का
recently *adv.* hāl meN हाल में
recognize (to) *v.t.* pahacānnā पहचानना
recommend (to) *v.t.* sifāriś karnā सिफ़ारिश करना
recommendation *n.* sifāriś *f.* सिफ़ारिश
red *adj.* lāl लाल
reflection *n.* cintan *m.* चिन्तन
refugee *n.* śaraṇārthī *m.* शरणार्थी
refund (to) *v.t.* lauṭānā लौटाना
region *n.* ilāqā *m.* इलाक़ा
regret (to) *v.t.* pachtānā पछताना
relaxation *n.* ārām *m.* आराम
relief (from burden) *n.* chuṭkārā *m.* छुटकारा
religion *n.* dharm *m.* धर्म
religious *adj.* dhārmik धार्मिक
remember (to) *v.t.* yād karnā याद करना
remembrance *n.* yād *f.* याद

rent (to) *v.t.* kirāye par lenā किराये पर लेना
republic *n.* gaṇtantra *m.* गणतंत्र
research *n.* śodh *m.* शोध
research (to) *v.t.* śodh karnā शोध करना
reservation *n.* ārkṣaṇ *m.* आरक्षण
reserve (to reserve a room, seat, etc.) *v.t.* ārkṣit karnā आरक्षित करना
residence *n.* nivās *m.* निवास
respect *n.* ādar *m.* आदर
rest *n.* ārām *m.* आराम
rest (remainder) *n.* bākī *f.* बाकी
restaurant *n.* restarāN *m.* रेस्तराँ
return (to) *v.i.* lauṭnā लौटना
revenge *n.* badlā *m.* बदला
review (literary) *n.* samīkṣā *f.* समीक्षा
rhythm *n.* tāl *m.* ताल
rice (cooked) *n.* bhāt *m.* भात
rice (uncooked) *n.* cāval *m.* चावल
rich (in money) *adj.* dhanī / amīr धनी / अमीर
right (correct) *adj.* ṭhīk ठीक
right (direction) *adj.* dāhinā दाहिना
right now *adv.* abhī-abhī अभी-अभी
rights (civil) *n.* nāgrik adhikār *m.* नागरिक अधिकार
ring *n.* aNgūṭhī *f.* अँगूठी
risk *n.* jokhim *f.* जोखिम
river *n.* nadī *f.* नदी
road *n.* saṛak *f.* सड़क
rock *n.* caṭṭān *f.* चट्टान
rock climb (to) *v.t.* caṭṭānoN par caṛhnā चट्टानों पर चढ़ना
roof *n.* chat *f.* छत

room *n.* kamrā *m.* कमरा
room number *n.* kamre kā nambar *m.* कमरे का नमबर
rose *n.* gulāb *m.* गुलाब
round *adj.* gol गोल
rubbish *n.* kūṛā *m.* कूड़ा
rug *n.* galīcā *m.* गलीचा
ruins *n.* khanḍahar *m.* खंडहर
rule (regulation) *n.* niyam *m.* नियम
run (to) *v.i.* dauṛnā दौड़ना
run away (to) *v.i.* bhāg jānā भाग जाना
Russia *n.* rūs *m.* रूस
Russian *adj.* rūsī रूसी

S

sacred *adj.* pavitr पवित्र
sacrifice (rite) *n.* yāgya *m.* यज्ञ
sad *adj.* udās उदास
sadness *n.* udāsī *f.* उदासी
safe *adj.* surakṣit सुरक्षित
safe *n.* tijaurī *f.* तिजौरी
safety *n.* surakṣā *m.* सुरक्षा
saffron *n.* kesar *m.* केसर
saint (Hindu) *n.* sant *m.* संत
saint (Muslim) *n.* pīr *m.* पीर
salary *n.* tanqhvāh *f.* तनख़्वाह
sale *n.* bikrī *f.* बिक्री
salt *n.* namak *m.* नमक
salutation *n.* praṇām *m.* प्रणाम
same *adj.* samān समान

sand *n.* bālū *m.* बालू
sandalwood *n.* candan *m.* चंदन
satisfaction *n.* santoṣ *m.* संतोष
satisfied (to be) *v.i.* santoṣ honā संतोष होना
Saturday *n.* śanivār *m.* शनिवार
Saturn *n.* śani *m.* शनि
save (to) *v.t.* rakhnā रखना
save (to save a life) *v.t.* jān bacānā जान बचाना
say (to) *v.i. & v.t.* bolnā बोलना
scarf (women's) *n.* dupaṭṭā *m.* दुपट्टा
school *n.* vidhyālay *m.* विद्यालय
science *n.* vigyān *m.* विज्ञान
scientist *n.* vigyānī *m.* विज्ञानी
scissors *n.* katarnī *f.* कतरनी
screen *n.* pardā *m.* परदा
script (language) *n.* lipi *f.* लिपि
sculptor *n.* mūrtikār *m.* मूर्तिकार
sculpture *n.* mūrtikalā *f.* मूर्तिकला
sea *n.* samudr *m.* समुद्र
seaside *n.* samudrataṭ *m.* समुद्रतट
seat (chair) *n.* kursī *f.* कुर्सी
seatbelt *n.* kursī kī peṭī *f.* कुर्सी की पेटी
second *adj.* dūsrā दूसरा
see (to) *v.t.* dekhnā देखना
see you later! *interj.* phir mileNge! फिर मिलेंगे
selfish *adj.* svarthī स्वार्थी
sell (to) *v.t.* becnā बेचना
send (to) *v.t.* bhejnā भेजना
sentence (grammatical) *n.* vākya *m.* वाक्य
separate *adj.* alag अलग
separation *n.* vicched *m.* विच्छेद

series *n.* silsilā *m.* सिलसिला
serious *adj.* gambhīr गंभीर
service *n.* sevā *f.* सेवा
several *adj.* kaī कई
sew (to) *v.t.* silāī karnā सिलाई करना
sex (gender) *n.* ling *m.* लिंग
sexual intercourse *n.* sanbhog *m.* संभोग
shade *n.* chāyā *f.* छाया
shadow *n.* chāyā *f.* छाया
shampoo *n.* śaiNpū *m.* शैंपू
shape *n.* ākār *m.* आकार
share (to) *v.t.* bāNṭ denā बाँट देना
shave (to) *v.t.* mūNṛnā मूँड़ना
she *pron.* voh (at a distance) *f.* / yeh (nearby) *f.* वह / यह
sheep *n.* bheṛ *f.* भेड़
sheet (for bed) *n.* cādar *f.* चादर
sheet (of paper) *n.* qāqgaz *m.* क़ाग़ज़
shell (of nuts, etc.) *n.* chilkā *m.* छिल्का
ship *n.* jahāz *m.* जहाज़
shirt *n.* kamīz *f.* कमीज़
shoe *n.* jūtā *m.* जूता
shoe store *n.* jūte kī dukān *f.* जूते की दुकान
shop (to go shopping) *v.i.* kharīdārī karnā खरीदारी करना
shopkeeper *n.* dukāndār *m.* दुकानदार
short (length & height) *adj.* choṭā छोटा
shortage *n.* kamī *f.* कमी
shoulder *n.* kandhā *m.* कंधा
shout (to) *v.t.* cillānā चिल्लाना
show (spectacle) *n.* tamāśā *m.* तमाशा

show (to) *v.t.* dikhānā दिखाना
shower (to take a shower) *v.t.* phuhārā snān karnā फुहारा स्नान करना
shrine *n.* tīrth-mandir *m.* तीर्थ मंदिर
shut (to) *v.t.* band karnā बंद करना
sick *adj.* bīmār बीमार
sickness *n.* bīmārī *f.* बीमारी
sight *n.* dr̥ṣṭi *f.* दृष्टि
sign *n.* sanket *m.* संकेत
signature *n.* dastakhat *m.* दस्तखत
silence *n.* cuppī *f.* चुप्पी
silk *n.* reśm *m.* रेशम
silver *n.* cāNdī *f.* चाँदी
similar *adj.* samān समान
similarity *n.* samāntā *f.* समानता
simple *adj.* saral सरल
sin *n.* pāp *m.* पाप
sin (to) *v.i.* pāp karnā पाप करना
since *adv.* … se … से
sing (to) *v.t.* gānā गाना
singer *n.* gāyak *m.* / gāyikā *f.* गायक / गायिका
single (alone) *adj.* akelā अकेला
sister *n.* behn *f.* बहन
sit (to) *v.i.* baiṭhanā बैठना
situation *n.* sthiti *f.* स्थिति
skin (human) *n.* camṛī *f.* चमड़ी
sky *n.* ākāś *m.* आकाश
sleep *n.* nīnd *f.* नींद
sleep (to) *v.t.* sonā सोना
sleep well! *interj.* mastī soyeN! मस्ती सोयें
sleepy (to feel) *v.i.* nīnd ānā नींद आना

slowly *adv.* dhīre-dhīre धीरे-धीरे
smart (intelligent) *adj.* buddhimān बुद्धिमान
smell (bad odor) *n.* badbū *f.* बदबू
smell (good) *n.* qhuśbū *f.* ख़ुशबू
smell (to) *v.i. & v.t.* sūNghnā सूँघना
smile *n.* muskarāhaṭ *f.* मुस्कराहट
smile (to) *v.t.* muskarānā मुस्कराना
smoke (to smoke cigarettes) *v.t.* cigreṭ pīnā सिग्रेट पीना
snake *n.* sāNp *m.* साँप
soap *n.* sābun *m.* साबुन
soccer *n.* fuṭbāl *m.* फुटबाल
socialism *n.* samājvād *m.* समाजवाद
socialist *adj. & n.* samājvādī *m.* समाजवादी
social science *n.* sāmājik vigyān *m.* सामाजिक विग्यान
society *n.* samāj *m.* समाज
sock *n.* mozā *m.* मोज़ा
soft *adj.* mulāyam मुलायम
soldier *n.* sipāhī *m.* सिपाही
solid *adj.* ṭhos ठोस
some *adj.* kuch कुछ
somebody *pron.* koī *m.f.* कोई
something *pron.* kuch *m.f.* कुछ
sometimes *adv.* kabhī-kabhī कभी-कभी
somewhere *adv.* kahīN कहीं
son *n.* beṭā *m.* बेटा
song *n.* gānā *m.* गाना
soon *adj.* jaldī जल्दी
I'm sorry! *interj.* māf kījiye! माफ़ कीजिये
sound *n.* āvāz *f.* आवाज़

sour *adj.* khaṭṭā खट्टा
South *adj.* dakṣīṇ दक्षिण
souvenir *n.* niśānī *f.* निशानी
space *n.* jagah *f.* जगह
space (outer) *n.* antarikṣ *m.* अन्तरिक्ष
speak (to) *v.i. & v.t.* bolnā बोलना
special *adj.* khās / viśeṣ खास / विशेष
specialist *n.* viśeṣagya *m.* विशेषज्ञ
speech (formal) *n.* bhāṣṇ *m.* भाषण
speed *n.* cāl *f.* चाल
spices *n.* masāle *m.* मसाले
spicy (flavorful) *adj.* masāledār मसालेदार
spicy (hot) *adj.* tītā तीता
spider *n.* makṛī *f.* मकड़ी
spinach *n.* pālak *m.* पालक
spirit (soul) *n.* ātmā *m.* आत्मा
spiritual *adj.* ātmik आत्मिक
spoil (to overindulge) *v.t.* sir caṛhānā सिर चढ़ाना
spoon *n.* cammac *m.* चम्मच
spring (season) *n.* vasant *m.* वसंत
stairway *n.* sīṛhī *f.* सीढ़ी
stamp (postage) *n.* ṭikaṭ *m.* टिकट
standard of living *n.* jīvan star *m.* जीवन स्तर
star *n.* tārā *m.* तारा
start *v.t.* śurū karnā शुरू करना
statue *n.* mūrti *f.* मूर्ति
stay (to remain) *v.i.* rehnā रहना
step *n.* qadam *m.* क़दम
stomach *n.* peṭ *m.* पेट
stomachache *n.* peṭ kā dard *m.* पेट का दर्द
stone *n.* patthar *m.* पत्थर

stoned (from drugs) *adj.* naśe meN नशे में
stop (to) *v.i. & v.t.* roknā रोकना
storm *n.* tūfān *m.* तूफ़ान
story *n.* kahānī *f.* कहानी
stove *n.* cūlhā *m.* चूल्हा
straight *adj.* sīdhā सीधा
strange *adj.* ajīb अजीब
stranger *n.* ajnabī *m.* अजनबी
stream *n.* dhārā *f.* धारा
street *n.* saṛak *f.* सड़क
strength (bodily) *n.* bal *m.* बल
strike *n.* haṛtāl *f.* हड़ताल
string *n.* dhāgā *m.* धागा
strong *adj.* balī बली
stubborn *adj.* haṭhīlā हठीला
student *n.* vidyārthī *m.f.* विद्यार्थी
stupid (foolish) *adj.* mūrkh मूर्ख
style *n.* śailī *f.* शैली
suburb *n.* upnagar *m.* / muhallā *m.*
उपनगर / मुहल्ला
success *n.* saphaltā *f.* सफलता
successful *adj.* saphal सफल
suddenly *adj.* acānak अचानक
suffer (to) *v.i.* sahanā सहना
sugar *n.* cīnī *f.* चीनी
suicide *n.* ātmhatyā *f.* आत्महत्या
suitcase *n.* sūṭkes *m.* सूटकेस
summer *n.* garmī *f.* गरमी
sun *n.* sūrya *m.* सूर्य
sunburned (to become) *v.i.* dhūp se jalnā
धूप से जलना

Sunday *n.* ravivār *m.* रविवार
sunglasses *n.* dhūp kā caśmā *m.* धूप का चश्मा
sunlight *n.* dhūp *f.* धूप
sunrise *n.* sūryoday *m.* सूर्योदय
sunset *n.* sūryāst *m.* सूर्यास्त
support (to) *v.t.* sahārā denā सहारा देना
sure (certain) *adj.* niścit निश्चित
surgeon *n.* sarjan *m.* सर्जन
surname *n.* parivār kā nām *m.* परिवार का नाम
surprise *n.* āścarya *m.* आश्चर्य
survive (to) *v.i.* jīvit rehnā जीवित रहना
swallow (to) *v.t.* nigalnā निगलना
sweet *adj.* mīṭhā मीठा
sweet (candy) *n.* miṭhāī *f.* मिठाई
swim (to) *v.i.* tairnā तैरना
swimsuit *n.* tairne ke kapṛe *m.* तैरने के कपड़े
sword *n.* talvār *f.* तलवार
symbol *n.* pratīk *m.* प्रतीक
sympathetic *adj.* hamdard हमदर्द
sympathy *n.* hamdardī *f.* हमदर्दी
synagogue *n.* yahūdiyoN kā mandir *m.* यहूदियों का मंदिर

T

table *n.* mez *f.* मेज़
tailor *n.* darzī *m.* दर्ज़ी
take (to take away) *v.t.* le jānā ले जाना
take off (to) *v.i.* haṭānā हटाना
talented *adj.* pratibhāśālī प्रतिभाशाली
talk (to) *v.t.* bātcīt karnā बातचीत करना

tall *adj.* lambā लंबा
tampon *n.* ṭaimpān *m.* टैम्पॉन
target (objective) *n.* lakṣy *m.* लक्ष्य
taste *n.* svād *m.* स्वाद
tasty (delicious) *adj.* svādiṣṭ स्वादिष्ट
tax *n.* kar *m.* कर
taxi *n.* ṭaiksī *m.* टैक्सी
taxi stand *n.* ṭaiksī sṭaiNḍ *m.* टैक्सी स्टैंड
tea *n.* cāi *f.* चाय
teacher *n.* adhyāpak *m.* अध्यापक
teaching (education) *n.* śikṣā *f.* शिक्षा
team *n.* ṭīm *f.* टीम
technical *adj.* taknīkī तकनीकी
technique *n.* taknīk *m.* तकनीक
tedious *adj.* ubāū उबाऊ
telegram *n.* tār *m.* तार
telephone *n.* fon *m.* फ़ोन
telescope *n.* dūrbīn *m.* दूरबीन
television *n.* ṭelīvizan *f.* / ṭī vī *m.* टेलीविज़न / टी वी
tell (to) *v.t.* batānā बताना
temperature (fever) *n.* buqhār *m.* बुख़ार
temperature (outside) *n.* tāpmān *m.* तापमान
temple *n.* mandir *m.* मंदिर
temporary *adj.* asthāyī अस्थायी
tent *n.* tambū *m.* तंबू
terrace (balcony) *n.* chajjā *m.* छज्ज़ा
terrible *adj.* bhyankar भयंकर
test (exam) *n.* parīkṣā *f.* परीक्षा
testify (to) *v.t.* gavāhī denā गवाही देना
thank (to) *v.t.* dhanyavād denā धन्यवाद देना
thanks! *interj.inf.* śukriyā! शुक्रिया

thank you! *interj.for.* dhanyavād! धन्यवाद
that *conj.* ki कि
that *pron.* voh *m.f.* वह
theater *n.* thieṭar *m.* थिएटर
then *adv.* tab तब
there *adv.* wahāN वहाँ
therefore *adv.* isliye इसलिये
these *pron.* ye *m.f.* ये
they *pron.* ve (far) *m.f.* / ye (near) *m.f.* वे / ये
thick *adj.* moṭā मोटा
thief *n.* cor *m.* चोर
thin *adj.* patlā पतला
thing *n.* cīz *f.* चीज़
think (to) *v.t.* socnā सोचना
third *adj.* tīsrā तीसरा
thirsty (to be) *v.i.* pyās lagnā प्यास लगना
this *pron.* yeh *m.f.* यह
thought *n.* vicār *m.* विचार
throat *n.* galā *m.* गला
through *adv.* pār पार
thumb *n.* angūṭhā *m.* अंगूठा
Thursday *n.* guruvār *m.* गुउवार
ticket *n.* ṭikaṭ *m.* टिकट
tight *adj.* tang तंग
time *n.* samay *m.* समय
time (one time) *n.* ek bār *f.* एक बार
timetable *n.* samay sāriṇī *f.* समय सारिणी
tip (gratuity given usually in advance) *n.* baqhśīś *m.* बख़्शीश
tired (to become) *v.i.* thaknā थकना
to *prep.* ko को

tobacco *n.* tambākū *f.* तंबाकू
today *adv. & n.* āj *m.* आज
together *adv.* sāth sāth साथ साथ
toilet *n.* śaucālay *m.* शौचालय
toilet paper *n.* ṭāileṭ pepar *m.* टायलेट पेपर
tomorrow *adv. & n.* kal *m.* कल
tonight *adv. & n.* āj rāt *m.* आज रात
too (also) *adv.* bhī भी
too much / many *adj.* bahut zyādā बहुत ज़्यादा
tooth *n.* dāNt *m.* दाँत
toothache *n.* dāNt kā dard *m.* दाँत का दर्द
toothbrush *n.* dāNt kā braś *m.* दाँत का ब्रश
touch (to) *v.t.* chūnā छूना
tour *n.* sair *f.* सैर
tourist *n.* paryṭak *m.* पर्यटक
towards *adv.* … kī taraf … की तरफ़
towel *n.* tauliyā *m.* तौलिया
tower *n.* mīnār *f.* मीनार
town *n.* nagar *m.* नगर
toxic *adj.* viṣailā विषैला
tradition *n.* paramparā *f.* परम्परा
traditional *adj.* pāramparik पारम्परिक
traffic *n.* yātāyāt *m.* यातायात
trail (path) *n.* path *m.* पथ
train *n.* relgāṛī *f.* रेलगाड़ी
train station *n.* rel sṭeśan *m.* रेल स्टेशन
transit lounge *n.* pratīkṣālay *m.* प्रतीक्षालय
translate (to) *v.i. & v.t.* anuvād karnā अनुवाद करना
translation *n.* anuvād *m.* अनुवाद
transportation *n.* parivahan *m.* परिवहन
travel (to) *v.t.* yātrā karnā यात्रा करना

travel agency *n.* ṭraival ejenṭ *m.* ट्रैवल एजेंट
tree *n.* peṛ *m.* पेड़
trip *n.* yātrā *f.* यात्रा
trouble *adj. & n.* gaṛbaṛ *f.* गड़बड़
trousers *n.* patlūn *m.* पतलून
truck *n.* ṭrak *m.* ट्रक
true *adj.* sahī सही
truth *n.* saccāī *f.* सच्चाई
try (to attempt) *v.t.* kośiś karnā कोशिश करना
Tuesday *n.* mangalvār *m.* मंगलवार
tumor *n.* rasaulī *f.* रसौली
twice (*lit.* "two times") *adj.* do bār दो बार
twins *n.* juṛvāN *m.* जुड़वाँ
typical (common) *adj.* ām आम

U

ulcer *n.* phoṛā *m.* फोड़ा
umbrella *n.* chātā *m.* छाता
unbelievable *adj.* aviśvāsnīy अविश्वासनीय
uncertain (doubtful) *adj.* aniścit अनिश्चित
uncomfortable *adj.* beārām बेआराम
unconscious *adj.* behoś बेहोश
unconsciousness *n.* behośī *f.* बेहोशी
under *adv.* nīce नीचे
understand (to) *v.t.* samajhnā समझना
underwear *n.* andar ke kapṛe *m.* अन्दर के कपड़े
unemployment *n.* berozgārī *f.* बेरोज़गारी
unfortunately *adv.* durbhāgyavaś दुर्भाग्यवश
unhappy *adj.* dukhī दुखी
union (society) *n.* sangha *m.* संघ

universe *n.* viśva *m.* विश्व
university *n.* viśvavidhyālay *m.* विश्वविद्यालय
unknown *adj.* anjān अंजान
unmarried *adj.* avivāhit अविवाहित
unsafe *adj.* asurikṣit असुरक्षित
until (until …) *prep.* … tak … तक
unusual *adj.* asādhāraṇ असाधारण
up *adv.* ūpar ऊपर
urgent *adj.* bahut zarūrī बहुत ज़रूरी
urinate (to) *v.i.* peśāb karnā पेशाब करना
use *n.* prayog *m.* प्रयोग
use (to) *v.t.* istemāl karnā इस्तेमाल करना
useful *adj.* upyogī उपयोगी
useless *adj.* bekār बेकार
uterus *n.* garabhāśy *m.* गर्भाशय

V

vacant *adj.* qhālī ख़ाली
vacation *n.* chuṭṭī *f.* छुट्टी
vaccinate (to) *v.t.* ṭīkā lagānā टीका लगाना
vaccination *n.* ṭīkā *m.* टीका
vagina *n.* yoni *f.* योनि
valley *n.* ghāṭī *f.* घाटी
valuable *adj.* mūlyvān मूल्यवान
value (price) *n.* dām *m.* दाम
van *n.* band gāṛī *f.* बंद गाड़ी
various *adj.* tarah tarah तरह तरह
vegetable *n.* sabzī *f.* सब्ज़ी
vegetarian *adj.* *&* *n.* śākāhārī *m.* शाकाहारी
vegetarian food *n.* śākāhārī khānā *m.* शाकाहारी खाना

vegetation *n.* hariyālī *f.* हरियाली
vehicle *n.* gāṛī *f.* गाड़ी
veil *n.* pardā *m.* परदा
venereal disease *n.* gupt rog *m.* गुप्त रोग
very *adj.* bahut बहुत
victim *n.* śikār *m.* शिकार
view (scene) *n.* drśya *m.* दृश्य
village *n.* gāNv *m.* गाँव
vine *n.* bel *f.* बेल
vineyard *n.* angūr kā bāqg *m.* अंगूर का बाग़
violence *n.* himsā *f.* हिंसा
virus *n.* vāiras *m.* वाइरस
visa *n.* vīzā *m.* वीज़ा
visit (to) *v.i.* milne jānā मिलने जाना
visitor (guest) *n.* atithi *m.f.* अतिथि
vitamin *n.* viṭāmin *m.* विटामिन
vocabulary *n.* śabdāvalī *f.* शब्दावली
voice *n.* āvāz *f.* आवाज़
volunteer *n.* svayam sevak *m.* स्वयं सेवक
volunteer (to) *v.t.* svayam sevā karnā स्वयं सेवा करना
vomit *n.* ulṭī *f.* उलटी
vomit (to) *v.i.* ultī honā उलटी करना
vote (to) *v.t.* voṭ denā वोट देना
voyage *n.* yātrā *f.* यात्रा

W

wages *n.* tanqhvāh *f.* तनख़्वाह
wait (please wait!) *interj.* intazār kījiye! इंतज़ार कीजिये

wait (to) *v.i.* intazār karnā इंतज़ार करना
waiter *n.* bairā *m.* बैरा
wake up! *interj.* jāgo! जागो
wake up (to) *v.i.* jāgnā जागना
wake up (to wake someone up) *v.t.* jagānā जगाना
walk (to) *v.i.* paidal jānā पैदल जाना
wall *n.* dīvār *f.* दीवार
want (to) *v.t.* cāhnā चाहना
warm *adj.* garam गरम
warn (to) *v.t.* cetāvanī denā चेतावनी देना
warning *n.* cetāvanī *f.* चेतावनी
wash (to) *v.t.* dhonā धोना
wash (to bathe oneself) *v.i.* nahānā नहाना
waste *n.* kūṛā *m.* कूड़ा
watch (to observe) *v.t.* dekhnā देखना
water *n.* pānī *m.* पानी
water (mineral) *n.* minaral vāṭar *m.* मिनरल वॉटर
water bottle *n.* pānī kī botal *f.* पानी की बोतल
waterfall *n.* jharnā *m.* झरना
wave *n.* lahar *m.* लहर
way (path) *n.* rastā *m.* रास्ता
we *pron.* ham *m.f.* हम
weak *adj.* kamzor कमज़ोर
weakness *n.* kamzorī *f.* कमज़ोरी
wealthy *adj.* amīr अमीर
weapon *n.* śastr *m.* शस्त्र
wear (to) *v.t.* pehennā पहनना
weather *n.* mausam *m.* मौसम
wedding *n.* śādī *f.* शादी
Wednesday *n.* budhvār *m.* बुधवार
week *n.* haftā *m.* हफ़्ता

weigh (to) *v.i. & v.t.* tolnā तोलना
welcome! *interj.* svāgatam! स्वागतम
well (healthy) *adj.* tandurust तंदुरुस्त
West *n.* paścim *m.* पश्चिम
wet *adj.* gīlā गीला
what *interr.* kyā क्या
whatever *adv.* jo bhī जो भी
wheat *n.* gehūN *m.* गेहूँ
wheel *n.* cakr *m.* चक्र
wheelchair *n.* vhīl caiyar *m.* व्हील चैयर
when *adv.* kab कब
whenever *adv.* jab bhī जब भी
where *conj. & interr.* jahāN जहाँ; kahāN कहाँ
wherever *adv.* kahīN bhī कहीं भी
which *adj.* kaun कौन
white *adj.* safed सफ़ेद
white (Caucasian) *adj.* gorā गोरा
who *pron.* kaun *m.f.* कौन
whole (all) *adj.* pūrā पूरा
why *interr.* kyoN क्यों
wide *adj.* cauṛā चौड़ा
widow *n.* vidhvā *f.* विधवा
wife *n.* patnī *f.* पत्नी
win (to) *v.t.* jītnā जीतना
wind *n.* havā *f.* हवा
window *n.* khiṛkī *f.* खिड़की
wine *n.* śarāb *f.* शराब
wing *n.* pankha *m.* पंख
winner *n.* vijetā *m.* विजेता
winter *n.* jāṛā *m.* जाड़ा
wise *adj.* buddhimān बुद्धिमान

with *prep.* … ke sāth … के साथ
within *adv.* andar अन्दर
without *adv.* … ke binā … के बिना
wolf *n.* bheṛiyā *m.* भेड़िया
woman *n.* aurat *f.* औरत
wood *n.* lakṛī *f.* लकड़ी
wool *n.* ūn *m.* ऊन
word *n.* śabd *m.* शब्द
work *n.* kām *m.* काम
work (to) *v.t.* kām karnā काम करना
world *n.* sansār *m.* संसार
worm *n.* kīṛā *m.* कीड़ा
worry *n.* cintā *f.* / pareśān *m.* चिन्ता / परेशान
worry (to) *v.t.* cintā karnā चिन्ता करना
worship (to) *v.t.* pūjā karnā पूजा करना
wound *n.* ghāv *m.* घाव
write (to) *v.t.* likhnā लिखना
writer *n.* lekhak *m.* लेखक
wrong *adj.* qgalat ग़लत

X

xenophobia *n.* videśī dveṣ *m.* विदेशी द्वेष
x-ray *n.* eks re *m.* एक्स रे

Y

yawn *n.* janbhāī *f.* जंभाई
yawn (to) *v.i.* janbhāī lenā जंभाई लेना
year *n.* sāl *m.* साल
yeast *n.* khamīr *m.* खमीर

yell (to) *v.t.* cillānā चिल्लाना
yes! *interj.* hāN! हाँ
yesterday *n.* kal *m.* कल
yet *adv.* abhī tak अभी तक
yogurt *n.* dahī *m.* दही
you *pron.fam.* tum *m.f.* तुम
you *pron.for.* āp *m.f.* आप
young *adj.* javān जवान
yourself *pron.* āp svayam *m.f.* आप स्वयं
youth *n.* javānī *f.* जवानी

Z

zebra *n.* zebrā *m.* ज़ेबरा
zero *n.* śūnya *m.* शून्य
zodiac *n.* rāśi cakra *f.* राशी चक्र
zoo *n.* ciṛryāghar *m.* चिड़ियाघर

Hindi Phrasebook

Greetings & Politeness

Hello
नमस्ते
namaste *inf.*

नमस्कार
namaskār *for.*

What is your name?
आप का नाम क्या है ।
āp kā nām kyā hai?

My name is Rām.
मेरा नाम राम है ।
merā nām rām hai.

I am very happy to meet you.
आप से मिल कर मुझे बहुत ख़ुशी हुई ।
āp se milkar mujhe bahut qhuśī huī.

How are you?
आप कैसे हैं ।
āp kaise haiN?

I am fine, and you?
मैं ठीक हूँ और आप ।
maiN ṭhīk hūN aur āp?

Where are you from?
आप कहाँ से हैं ।
āp kahāN se haiN?

I am from America, and you?
मैं अमरीका से हूँ और आप ।
maiN amrīkā se hūN aur āp?

This is my friend. His name is Bill.
यह मेरा दोस्त है । इस का नाम बिल है ।
yeh merā dost hai. is kā nām bil hai.

What is his / her name?
उस का नाम क्या है ।
us kā nām kyā hai?

What type of work do you do?
आप क्या काम करते हैं ।
āp kyā kām karte haiN?

I am a student.
मैं विद्यार्थी हूँ ।
maiN vidyārṭhī hūN.

Family

Are you married?
क्या आप शादी शुदा हैं ।
kyā āp śādī śudā haiN?

How many siblings do you have?
आप के कितने भाई-बहन हैं ।
āp ke kitne bhāī behen haiN?

Note: Familial relationships and responsibility for the extended family are extremely important in India. Also, friends are valued like family in India. Even as a foreigner, once you become close to an Indian family you will be treated as a family member. In a typical household, friends and extended family will come by unannounced and be offered dinner, etc. People tend to share more with each other and are not as possessive of their personal space and privacy as Americans can be.

I have. . . .
मेरा *m.s.* / मेरी *f.s.pl.* / मेरे *m.pl.for*. . . . है *s.* / हैं *pl.* ।
mera *m.s.* / meri *f.s.pl.* / mere *m.pl.for*. . . . hai *s.* / haiN *pl.*

brother
भाई
bhāī

sister
बहन
behen

older brother
बड़ा भाई
baṛa bhāī

younger brother
छोटा भाई
choṭa bhāī

older sister
बड़ी बहन
baṛī behen

younger sister
छोटी बहन
choṭī behen

son
बेटा
beṭā

daughter
बेटी
beṭī

husband
पति
pati

wife
पत्नी
patnī

grandmother (maternal)
नानी
nānī

grandfather (maternal)
नाना
nānā

grandmother (paternal)
दादी
dādī

grandfather (paternal)
दादा
dādā

aunt (maternal)
मामी
māmī

uncle (maternal)
मामा
māmā

aunt (paternal)
चाची
cācī

uncle (paternal)
चाचा
cācā

Expressing Emotions & Needs

I need / want some water.
मुझे पानी चाहिये ।
mujhe pānī cāhiye.

I need to buy some water.
मुझे पानी खरीदना है ।
mujhe pānī kharīdnā hai.

Note: You are highly advised to drink only bottled water while in India. Several companies such as Bisleri and Aquafina have their brands for sale in India. Some of the nicer hotels and restaurants will have water-filtering systems, but even in those cases you should drink only bottled water. You also can request boiled water at your hotel or use water-purification pills in tap water. In general, the Indian *chai* or spiced tea is safe to drink as it has been boiled with the milk before serving. Also, bottled soft drinks are safe and available everywhere. It is also best to request drinks "without ice" when ordering in a restaurant.

I am very tired.
मैं बहुत थका हूँ ।
maiN bahut thakā hūN.

I am getting sleepy.
मुझे नींद आ रही है ।
mujhe nīnd ā rahī hai.

I am angry.
मैं गुस्सा में हूँ ।
maiN gussā meN hūN.

I feel sad.
मुझे उदासी लगती है ।
mujhe udāsī lagtī hai.

I feel stressed.
मुझे तनाव लगता है ।
mujhe tanāv lagtā hai.

I feel hungry.
मुझे भूख लगी ।
mujhe bhūkh lagī.

I am worried.
मैं चिंता में हूँ ।
maiN cintā meN hūN.

I am very happy.
मैं बहुत ख़ुश हूँ ।
maiN bahut qhuś hūN.

I like this one.
मुझे यह पसंद है ।
mujhe yeh pasand hai.

I don't like this.
मुझे यह पसंद नहीं है ।
mujhe yeh pasand nahīN hai.

That's enough!
बस ।
bas!

I have to go to. . . .
मुझे . . . जाना है ।
mujhe . . . jānā hai.

That is fine / OK.
वह तो ठीक है ।
voh to ṭhīk hai.

That is not fine / OK.
वह ठीक नहीं है ।
voh ṭhīk nahīN hai.

OK, I have to go now. See you later!
अच्छा मुझे जाना है । फिर मिलेंगे ।
acchā, mujhe jānā hai. phir mileNge!

Do you know English?
क्या आप को अंग्रेज़ी आती है ।
kyā āp ko aNgrezī ātī hai?

I can speak only a little bit of Hindi.
मैं थोड़ी सी हिन्दी बोल सकता *m.* / सकती *f.* हूँ ।
maiN thoṛī sī hindī bol saktā *m.* / saktī *f.* hūN.

How do you say . . . in Hindi?
हिन्दी में . . . कैसे कहते हैं ।
hindī meN . . . kaise kahate haiN?

Please speak slowly.
ज़रा धीरे धीरे बोलिये ।
zarā dhīre dhīre boliye.

Please say it again.
फिर से बोलिये ।
phir se boliye.

This is very good, isn't it?
यह बहुत अच्छा है, ना ।
yeh bahut acchā hai, nā?

Not now.
अभी नहीं ।
abhī nahīN.

Not yet.
अभी तक नहीं ।
abhī ṭak nahīN.

Please come later on.
बाद में आईये ।
bād meN āīye.

I like India very much.
मुझे भारत बहुत अच्छा लगता है ।
mujhe bhārat bahut acchā lagtā hai.

I am running late.
मुझे देर हो रही है ।
mujhe der ho rahī hai.

I understand.
मैं समझता *m.* / समझती *f.* हूँ।
maiN samajhtā *m.* / samajhtī *f.* hūN.

Do you understand?
क्या आप समझते हैं।
kyā āp samajhte haiN?

Asking For Directions

Excuse me (*lit.* "please listen"), where is the. . . ?
सुनिये,. . . कहाँ है ।
suniye, . . . kahāN hai?

airport
हवाई अड्डा
havāī aḍḍā

bank
बैंक
baiNk

bus station
बस का अड्डा
bas kā aḍḍā

chemist (pharmacy)
दवा खाना
davā khānā

market
बाज़ार
bāzār

museum
संग्रहालय
sangrahālay

police station
थाना
thānā

post office
डाक घर
ḍāk ghar

restroom
शौचालय
śaucālay

train station
रेल्वे सटेशन
relve sṭeśan

How far is it from here?
यहाँ से कितनी दूर है ।
yahāN se kitnī dūr hai?

It is not far.
बहुत दूर नहीं है ।
bahut dūr nahīN hai.

It is very near.
बहुत पास है ।
bahut pās hai.

Which street is this?
यह कौनसी सड़क है ।
yeh kaunsī saṛak hai?

Go straight.
सीधे जाइये ।
sīdhe jāiye.

Straight ahead.
सीधे आगे ।
sīdhe āge.

Turn left / turn right.
बायें तरफ़ मुड़िये / दायें तरफ़ मुड़िये ।
bāyeN taraf muṛiye / dāyeN taraf muṛiye.

You'll find it on the left-hand side.
बाईं तरफ़ मिलेगा ।
bāyīN taraf milegā.

You'll find it on the right-hand side.
दाईं तरफ़ मिलेगा ।
dāīN taraf milegā.

It is directly across from the shoe store.
जूते की दुकान के ठीक सामने है ।
jūte kī dukān ke ṭhīk sāmne hai.

It will take [10] minutes by rickshaw (three-wheel taxi).
रिक्शा से [दस] मिनट लगेंगे ।
rikśā se [das] minaṭ lagenge.

North
उत्तर
uttar

South
दक्षीण
dakṣīṇ

East
पूर्व
pūrva

West
पश्चिम
paścim

in between
बीच में
bīc meN

behind X
x के पीछे
X ke pīche

in front of X
x के सामने
X ke sāmne

Where are you going?
आप कहाँ जा रहे हैं ।
āp kahāN jā rehe haiN?

Please go safely.
सवधानी से जाइये ।
savdhānī se jāiye.

Travel & Transportation

Air Travel

You will find that English is widely spoken by airline and airport personnel in India. However, it will still be useful to know some key words and phrases. Airports in the North of India are good places to learn Hindi as most of the signs and announcements are given in Hindi and English. Be sure you know the correct airport for your flight. In New Delhi, for example, you will arrive from the U.S. and Europe at Indira Gandhi International Airport. However, when taking a domestic flight you will need to go to Delhi Palam airport which is next to the international airport. Taxi drivers will know it as "Palam" or "domestic airport." There is also a bus that travels between the two terminals.

Where is the airport?
हवाई अड्डा कहाँ है ।
havāī aḍḍā kahāN hai?

Is my flight delayed?
क्या मेरी उड़ान देर हो गयी है ।
kyā merī uṛān der ho gayī hai?

Flight number [420] has been delayed.
उड़ान [420] देर हो गयी है ।
uṛān [420] der ho gayī hai.

Flight number [420] has been cancelled.
उड़ान [420] कैंसिल हो गयी है ।
uṛān [420] kaiNsil (cancel) ho gayī hai.

Where is the domestic terminal?
देशीय टर्मिनल कहाँ है ।
deśīy ṭerminal kahāN hai?

Where is the bus to the domestic terminal?
देशीय टर्मिनल जाने वाली बस कहाँ से मिलेगी ।
deśīy ṭerminal jāne vālī bas kahāN se milegī?

I am taking Indian Airlines to Varanasi.
मैं इंडियन एयरलाइन्स से वाराणसी जा रहा *m.* / रही *f.* हूँ ।
maiN inḍiyan eyarlāins se Vārāṇasī jā rahā *m.* / rahī *f.* hūN.

I would like to make a reservation.
मुझे बुकिंग कराना है ।
mujhe buking karānā hai.

airport
हवाई अड्डा
havāī aḍḍā

domestic airport
देशीय हवाई अड्डा
deśīy havāī aḍḍā

international airport
अंतरराष्ट्रीय हवाई अड्डा
antarrāṣṭrīy havāī aḍḍā

airplane
विमान
vimān

arrival
आगमन
āgman

departure
प्रस्थान
prasthān

immigration
आवसन
āvasan

check-in counter
चेक इन काउंटर
cek in kāunṭar

boarding pass
प्रवेश पत्र
praveś patr

ticket
टिकट
ṭikaṭ

baggage check
सामान पत्र
sāmān patr

seat
सीट
sīṭ

baggage claim
सामान मिलने की जगह
sāmān milne kī jagah

delay
देर
der

flight number [67]
उड़ान [67]
uṛān [67]

information
सुचना
sūcnā

reservation
बुकिंग (or) आरक्षण
buking (or) ārakṣaṇ

reserve (to)
बुकिंग कराना
buking karānā

You might hear these phrases during your travels:

May I have your attention please.
कृपया ध्यान दीजिये ।
kripya dhyān dījiye.

We are about to land at [Varanasi].
हम [वाराणसी] पहुँचने वाले हैं ।
ham [vārāṇasī] pahuNcne wāle haiN.

Please fasten your seatbelt.
आप की कुर्सी की पेटी बांध लीजिये ।
āp kī kursī kī peṭī bāndh lījiye.

Please raise your tray table.
आप के ट्रे टेबल बंद रखें ।
āp ke ṭre ṭebal band rukheN.

We thank you for flying Indian Airlines.
हम आप को इंडियन एयरलाइन्स के साथ यात्रा करने के लिये बहुत धन्यवाद देते हैं ।
ham āp ko inḍiyan eyarlāins ke sāth yātrā karne ke liye bahut dhanyavād dete haiN.

We hope your journey was a pleasant one.
हमे आशा है कि आप की यात्रा सुखुशी हुई ।
hame āśā hai ki āp kī yātrā sukhuśī huī.

Thank you, goodbye.
धन्यवाद नमस्कार ।
dhanyavād, namaskār.

Bon voyage. (*lit.* "May you have an auspicious journey.")
आप की यात्रा मंगलमय हो ।
āp kī yātrā mangalmay ho.

Train

If you travel by train even once during your visit to India, it will be one of the most memorable parts of your experience in the country. The train system is extensive and hundreds of thousands of Indians travel by rail on a daily basis. You can book all of your tickets in advance at an Indian Railways booking office. Major cities such as New Delhi, Mumbai, Chennai and Kolkata will have large railway booking offices with special windows for tourists. If the train is fully booked you might be able to take advantage of a "tourist quota," which is often available. For most journeys, travel by first class or by air conditioned second class is recommended, when available. When traveling by train, be sure to lock your luggage to your berth while you sleep. You will have the opportunity to meet many interesting people and see the varied and beautiful landscapes of the Subcontinent from your window. If you travel by regular, non-air conditioned second class you will be able to see more of the land as the windows are not tinted. The food and beverages served by Indian Railways are usually quite fresh and tasty. If you are a woman traveling alone, by all means request to be seated in the "ladies' car." You will have a chance to talk with many Indian women and there will be a security guard at the end of the car.

When does the train to Varanasi leave?
वाराणसी जाने वाली गाड़ी कब छूटेगी ।
vārāṇasī jāne wālī gāṛī kab chūṭegī?

The train to Varanasi leaves in five minutes.
वाराणसी जाने वाली गाड़ी पाँच मिनट में छूटेगी ।
vārāṇasī jāne wālī gāṛī pāNc minat meN chūṭegī.

Please give me a second class a/c (air conditioned) ticket to Varanasi.
वाराणसी के लिये एक सेकंड किलास ए सी टिकट दीजिये ।
vārāṇasī ke liye ek sekaṇḍ kilās e. sī. ṭikaṭ dījiye.

From which platform does the train leave?
गाड़ी किस प्लेटफ़ार्म से छूटती है ।
gāṛī kis pleṭfārm se chūṭtī hai?

The train leaves from platform number [one].
गाड़ी [एक] नमबर प्लेटफ़ार्म से छूटती है ।
gāṛī [ek] nambar pleṭfārm se chūṭtī hai.

Does this train stop in Allahabad?
क्या यह गाड़ी इलाहबाद रूकती है ।
kyā yeh gāṛī ilāhabād rūktī hai?

What time will we reach Varanasi?
हम वाराणसी कितने बजे पहुँचेंगे ।
ham vārāṇasī kitne baje pahuNchenge?

Is the train late?
क्या गाड़ी देर हो गयी है ।
kyā gāṛī der ho gayī hai?

How much is a platform ticket?
प्लेटफ़ार्म टिकट का दाम क्या है ।
pleṭfārm ṭikaṭ kā dām kyā hai?

Note: A platform ticket is needed if you want to go onto the platform to see someone off or to meet someone. Seeing someone off at the airport or train station is very important in Indian culture.

Excuse me, where is the waiting room?
सुनिये, प्रतीक्षालय कहाँ है ।
suniye, pratīkṣālay kahāN hai?

I need a porter.
मुझे कुली चाहिये ।
mujhe kulī cāḥiye.

I don't need a porter.
मुझे कुली नहीं चाहिये ।
mujhe kulī nahīN cāhiye.

train station
रेलवे स्टेशन
relve sṭeśan

reservation desk
आरक्षण काउंटर
ārakṣaṇ kaunṭar

railway timetable
रेलवे टाईम टेबल
relve ṭāīm ṭebal

reserved coach
आरक्षित कोच
ārakṣit koc

first class
प्रथम श्रेणी
pratham śreṇī

second class
द्वितीय श्रेणी
dvitīy śreṇī

berth
बिर्थ
birth

waiting room
विश्राम कक्ष
viśrām kakṣ

conductor
संवाहक
saṃvāhak

station master
स्टेशन मास्टर
sṭeśan māsṭar

arrival
आगमन
āgman

departure
प्रस्थान
prasthān

exit
निर्गम
nirgam

Bus

Bus travel in India can be quite an adventure. For long distances, it is definitely not recommended. However, for journeys of a few hours or within a city or town, buses can be an inexpensive and convenient way to get around. Be aware that local buses can be crowded beyond capacity making even a short journey uncomfortable. In most cases you should just get on the bus and buy your ticket from the attendant.

Excuse me, where is the [bus stop] / [bus station]?
सुनिये [बस स्टाप] / [बस का अड्डा] कहाँ है ।
suniye, [bas sṭāp] / [bas kā aḍḍā] kahāN hai?

Excuse me, which bus is going to [Shirdi]?
ज़रा सुनिये [शिड़ी] जाने वाली बस कौनसी है ।
zarā suniye, [śirḍī] jāne vālī bas kaunsī hai?

It will be here in five minutes.
पाँच मिनट में आयेगी ।
pāNc minaṭ meN āyegī.

Where can I buy a ticket?
टिकट कहाँ खरीद सकता *m.* / सकती *f.* हूँ ।
ṭikaṭ kahāN kharīd saktā *m.* / saktī *f.* hūN?

You can buy the ticket on the bus.
आप बस पर खरीद सकते हैं ।
āp bas par kharīd sakte haiN.

What is the fare to [Shirdi]?
[शिर्ड़ी] जाने का किराया कितने का है ।
[śirḍī] jāne kā kirāyā kitne kā hai?

We are going to [Shirdi]. Please tell us when we need to get off.
हम [शिर्ड़ी] जा रहे हैं । हम को बताइयेगा कि हम कहाँ उतरें ।
ham [śirḍī] jā rahe haiN. ham ko batāiyegā kī ham kahāN utareN.

Is this seat taken?
क्या यह सीट ख़ाली है ।
kyā yeh sīṭ qhālī hai?

Taxi & Rickshaw (Three-Wheel Taxi)

You will find auto rickshaws (three-wheel scooter taxis) and bicycle rickshaws all over India. Be sure to negotiate your fare before you get in the vehicle. Drivers rarely will use the meter. Even if they do, the meters are often outdated and they will show you a fare increase card. Bicycle rickshaws will of course have no meter and always must be negotiated. If you are unsure about how much you should be charged, ask at the hotel desk. Regular taxis will be more expensive and you can usually insist that the driver use the meter. You can also rent a taxi for many hours or for a day of sightseeing. Be careful when negotiating a fare to the airport as this is often a fixed price. Also, if you are traveling at night, drivers often will include a "night charge" in your fare. In general, there is no practice of tipping drivers. However, if the driver carries your bags or you spend the day with him sightseeing, you can tip at your discretion.

How much is the fare to the [Baha'i temple]?
[बहाई टेम्पल] जाने के कितने पैसे लगते हैं ।
[bahāī ṭempal] jāne ke kitne paise lagte haiN?

Please use the meter.
मीटर इस्तेमाल कीजिये ।
mīṭar istemāl kījiye.

That is too much. Last time it was only 100 rupees.
यह ज़्यादा है । पिछली बार केवल सौ रुपये थे ।
yeh zyādā hai. pichlī bār keval sau rupaye the.

I'll give you only 125 rupees.
मैं सिर्फ़ एक सौ पच्चीस दूँगा *m.* / दूँगी *f.* ।
maiN sirf ek sau paccīs dūNgā *m.* / dūNgī *f.*

Please stop here.
यहाँ रूक जाइये ।
yahāN rūk jāiye.

How much is it to go round trip to [Sarnath]?
[सारनाथ] जाने आने के कितने पैसा लगेंगे ।
[sārnāth] jāne āne ke kitne paise lagenge?

Excuse me, where can I get a taxi / rickshaw?
सुनिये टैक्सी / रिक्शा कहाँ मिलेगी ।
suniye, ṭaiksī / rikshā kahāN milegī?

Please take me to this address.
कृपया मुझे इस पते पर ले चलिये ।
kripya mujhe is pate par le caliye.

Accommodation

You will find a wide range of accommodations in India; from dormitory-type hostels for around five U.S. dollars per night, to five-star luxury hotels that can be 400 U.S. dollars per night or more. Whatever your budget, you will find accommodation to your liking. Consult a current guidebook that has updated and specific information on hotels. You also can learn a lot from talking with other travelers as they can recommend or not recommend a place from their previous stops. For the more expensive hotels, booking in advance is recommended. Since your flight from the U.S. or Europe most likely will be arriving very late at night, you might want to book a room at a decent hotel for at least the first night or two while you adjust to your surroundings.

I am looking for a clean and inexpensive hotel.
मैं साफ़ और सस्ता होटल ढूँढ रहा *m.* / रही *f.* हूँ ।
maiN sāf aur sasta hoṭal ḍūNḍ (rahā *m.* /
rahī *f.)* hūN.

What is the address?
पता क्या है ।
patā kyā hai?

Please write down the address for me in Hindi.
ज़रा हिन्दी में पता लिख दीजिये ।
zarā hindi meN patā likh dījiye.

Do you have any rooms available?
कोई कमरा खाली है ।
koī kamrā khālī hai?

for only one night
सिर्फ़ एक रात के लिये
sirf ek rāt ke liye

Is breakfast included?
क्या नाश्ता किराये में शामिल है ।
kyā nāśtā kirāye meN śāmil hai?

I have a reservation.
मेरी जगह रखी है ।
merī jagah rakhī hai.

Do you have any single rooms / double rooms available?
कोई सिंगल कमरा / डबल कमरा मिलेगा ।
koī siṇgal kamra / ḍabal kamra milegā?

We need two beds.
हम को दो पलंग चाहिये ।
ham ko do palang cāhiye.

What is the rate (*lit.* "rent") per night?
एक दिन का किराया कितना है ।
ek din kā kirāyā kitnā hai?

It's [Rs. 200] per night.
एक दिन का किराया [दो सौ रुपय] हैं ।
ek din kā kirāyā [do sau rupaye] haiN.

First show me the room, then I will decide.
कमरा दिखाइये फिर मैं फ़ैसला करूँगा *m.* / करूँगी *f.* ।
kamrā dikhāiye phir maiN faislā karūNgā *m.* / karūNgī *f.*

Note: It is perfectly acceptable at smaller hotels or guest houses to ask to see the room before you decide.

This room is not good. Please show me another one.
यह कमरा ठीक नहीं है । दूसरा कमरा दिखाइये ।
yeh kamrā ṭhīk nahīN hai. dūsrā kamrā dikhāiye.

I'll take this room.
यह कमरा ले लूँगा *m.* / लूँगी *f.* ।
yeh kamrā le lūNgā *m.* / lūNgī *f.*

Please wake me at 9 A.M.
ज़रा नौ बजे मुझे उठा दीजियेगा ।
zarā nau baje mujhe uṭhā dījiyegā.

Do you have a mosquito net?
मच्छरदानी आप के पास है ।
macchardānī āp ke pās hai?

Note: Most smaller hotels without air conditioning will have sturdy ceiling fans in each room. Keeping your fan on a high setting at night is the best way to keep mosquitos from buzzing in your ears. You might want to bring a strong insect repellant with you from home as well. Mosquito coils, although deemed unsafe in the U.S., are still available in India and are effective if you have no alternative.

Has anyone called?
कोई फ़ोन आया है ।
koī fon āyā hai?

I'm leaving at [two o'clock].
मैं [दो बजे] जा रहा *m.* / रही *f.* हूँ ।
maiN [do baje] jā rahā *m.* / rahī *f.* hūN.

I'd like to pay my bill.
बिल दे दीजिये ।
bil de dījiye.

I want to speak to the manager.
मैं मैनेजर से बोलना चाहता *m.* / चाहती *f.* हूँ ।
maiN mainejar se bolnā cāhatā *m.* / cāhatī *f.* hūN.

I need. . . .
मुझे . . . चाहिये ।
mujhe . . . cāhiye.

lightbulb
बल्ब
balb

candles
मोमबत्ती
mombattī

matches
माचिस
mācis

electricity
बिजली
bijalī

food
खाना
khānā

soap
साबुन
sābun

towel
तौलिया
tauliyā

clean sheets
साफ़ चादर
sāf cādar

key
चाभी
cābhī

hot water
गरम पानी
garam pānī

boiled water
उब्ला हुआ पानी
ublā huā pānī

pillow
तकिया
takiyā

pillowcase
तकिये का ख़ोल
takiye kā qhol

blanket
कम्बल
kambal

Food & Drink

At the Restaurant

India has one of the most complex and diverse cuisines in the world. Whether you indulge in the hearty Moghul cuisine of the North or the delectable vegetarian food of the South, you will undoubtedly miss these foods after returning home.

Can you recommend a good restaurant?
क्या आप एक अच्छा रेस्तराँ बता सकते हैं ।
kyā āp ek acchā restarāN batā sakte haiN?

Can you recommend an inexpensive restaurant?
क्या आप एक सस्ता रेस्तराँ बता सकते हैं ।
kyā āp ek sastā restarāN batā sakte haiN?

I am a vegetarian.
मैं शाकाहारी हूँ ।
maiN śākāhārī hūN.

I am not a vegetarian. He / She is a vegetarian.
मैं शाकाहारी नहीं हूँ । वह शाकाहारी है ।
maiN śākāhārī nahīN hūN. voh śākāhārī hai.

Is this food vegetarian?
क्या यह खाना शाकाहारी है ।
kyā yeh khānā śākāhārī hai?

Do you have any. . . ?
कोई . . . आप के पास है ।
koī . . . āp ke pās hai?

Please give me a. . . .
मुझे एक़ . . . दे दीजिये ।
mujhe ek . . . de dījiye.

I don't eat meat.
माँस नहीं खाता *m.* / खाती *f.* हूँ ।
māNs nahīN khātā *m.* / khātī *f.* hūN.

I don't eat pork.
सूअर का गोश्त नहीं खाता *m.* / खाती *f.* हूँ ।
sūar kā gośt nahīN khātā *m.* / khātī *f.* hūN.

I don't eat beef.
गोमाँस नहीं खाता *m.* / खाती *f.* हूँ ।
gomāNs nahīN khātā *m.* / khātī *f.* hūN.

What kind of meat is this?
यह किस तरह का माँस है ।
yeh kis tarah kā māNs hai?

This doesn't seem fresh.
यह ताज़ा नहीं लगता ।
yeh tāzā nahīN lagtā.

I don't want any ice.
मुझे बर्फ़ नहीं चाहिये ।
mujhe barf nahīN cāhiye.

This food is excellent!
खाना कमाल का है ।
khānā kamāl kā hai!

delicious!
स्वादिष्ट ।
svādiṣṭ!

Is there garlic in this?
क्या इस में लहसुन है ।
kyā is meN lahasun hai?

Please bring me the bill.
कृपया बिल ले आइये ।
kripā bil le āiye.

This is not clean.
यह साफ़ नहीं है ।
yeh sāf nahīN hai.

This is too cold.
यह ज़्यादा ठण्डा है ।
yeh zyādā ṭhaṇḍā hai.

I am allergic to. . . .
मुझे . . . से एलरगी है ।
mujhe . . . se elargī hai.

without chili peppers
मिर्च के बिना ।
mirc ke binā

without spices
मसाले के बिना
masāle ke binā

Please do not make the food too spicy (hot).
ज़रा बहुत कम मिर्च डालिये ।
zarā bahut kam mirc ḍāliye.

breakfast
नाश्ता
nāśtā

lunch
दिन का खाना
din kā khānā

dinner / supper
रात का खाना
rāt kā khānā

menu
मेन्यू
menyū

glass
गिलास
gilās

cup
प्याला
pyālā

plate
प्लेट
pleṭ

spoon
चम्मच
cammac

knife
चाकू
cākū

paper napkin
पेपर नैपकिन
pepar naipkin

Food

Breads

naan: unleavened bread made in the tandūr (traditional clay oven)
नान
nān

chapati: unleavened wheat bread made over an open flame
चपाती
capātī

paratha: unleavened griddle bread, shallow-fried in a skillet, often stuffed with potatoes, cheese, etc.
पराठा
parāṭhā

puri: unleavened wheat bread that puffs when fried
पूड़ी
pūṛī

Fruit
फल
phal

Fruit sellers and fruit are plentiful in India. Eating oranges is a great way to stay hydrated during the hot months. It is best to eat fruit that you can peel such as bananas and oranges. For other fruits and vegetables, be sure to wash them with bottled or purified water.

mango
आम
ām

banana
केला
kelā

apple
सेब
seb

grapes
अँगूर
aNgūr

oranges
संतरे
santre

Vegetables
सबज़ियाँ
sabziyāN

onion
प्याज़
pyāz

tomatoes
टमाटर
ṭamāṭar

cucumber
खीरा
khīrā

garlic
लहसुन
lehsun

Appetizers / Snacks
हल्का नाश्ता
halkā nāśtā

vegetable pakoras: batter-fried vegetables served with chutney
सब्ज़ी पकौड़ा
sabzī pakauṛā

cheese pakoras: batter-fried cheese served with chutney
पनीर पकौड़ा
panīr pakauṛā

samosas: pastry-like snacks filled with potatoes, peas, spices, etc.
समोसे
samose

papad: crispy fried lentil wafer served with chutney
पापड़
pāpaṛ

masala dosa: flat like a crepe, and stuffed with potatoes, etc. Served with coconut chutney and sambar.
मसाला दोसा
masālā dosā

omelette
आमलेट
āmleṭ

toast
टोस्ट
ṭosṭ

Vegetarian Entrees
सब्ज़ियों के परोसे
sabziyoN ke parose

baigan bharta: smoked eggplant
बैंगन भरता
baiNgan bhartā

palak paneer: creamed spinach and cheese
पालक पनीर
pālak panīr

chana masala: chickpeas in gravy
चना मसाला
canā masālā

aloo gobhi: potato cauliflower curry
आलू गोभी
ālū gobhī

daal: cooked lentils with spices
दाल
dāl

matar paneer: peas and cheese
मटर पनीर
maṭar panīr

vegetarian thali
शाकाहारी थाली
śākāhārī thālī

A thālī is a large plate with individual sections on it for various types of food. It can also be a large, round plate with smaller bowls on it. A vegetarian thali might include rice, papad, various curries, dal, papadams and accompaniments. A "veg thālī" or "non-veg thālī" is a great way to sample the savory food of India. In the South of India, you might have your thālī dish served on a banana leaf.

malai kofta: dumplings made from various vegetables, cooked in a cream sauce
मलाई कोफ़्ता
malāī koftā

Non-Vegetarian Entrees
माँसाहारी परोसे
māNsāhārī parose

chicken tikka: boneless pieces of chicken slow-cooked with spices in the traditional Indian clay oven (tandūr)
मुर्गी टिक्का
murgī ṭikkā

tandoori chicken: chicken cooked in a tandūr oven, served with onions and chutney
तंदूरी मुर्गी
tandūrī murgī

mutton curry
रोगन जोश
rogan jośa

kebabs
सीख कबाब
sīkh kabāb

Rice Dishes

biryani: rice layered with vegetables or meat, cooked in spices
बिरयानी
biryānī

pulao: fluffy rice dish cooked with spices and vegetables such as peas
पुलाव
pulāv

Side Dishes / Accompaniments
अन्य खाने की चीज़े
anya khāne kī cīze

mango pickle
अचार
acār

raita: cucumber yogurt
रायता
raitā

Drinks
पेय
pey

You will find a variety of soft drinks in India such as Coca-Cola, Pepsi, and many excellent Indian brands. Bottled beers such as Kingfisher and other Indian brands also are available and safe to drink. For a refreshing change you can order "fresh lime sodas" at restaurants, which is plain soda water served with fresh-squeezed lime juice and sugar syrup on the side. Delicious spiced Indian tea *(chai)* is available everywhere.

lassi: a yogurt drink that can be made sweet, salty, with mangos, etc.
लस्सी
lassī

soft drinks
ठण्डे
ṭhaṇḍe

tea
चाय
cāi

Sweets
मिठाइयाँ
miṭhāiyāN

The best way to learn which sweets you will like is to try them. You can go into any sweet shop and get a sample of sweets packaged in a nice little box. These sweets are unique in flavor as most are made with solid milk as a base. They are delicious when eaten with tea. Below are short descriptions of only a few common sweets. You will see hundreds of varieties, especially during festivals.

jalebi: deep-fried, orange or gold in color, pretzel-shaped, crispy, best eaten only when fresh
जलेबी
jalebī

kulfi: Indian "ice cream" made from milk that is flavored with pistachios, mangos or almonds

कुल्फ़ी

kulfī

barfi: this is a very common sweet, made from solidified milk. Barfi comes in many flavors including pistachio and almond.

बर्फ़ी

barfī

gulab jamun: a round, brown-colored sweet soaked in sweet syrup and rose water

गुलाब जामुन

gulāb jāmun

khir: a delicious rice pudding made with milk, cashews and raisins. This can be served warm or chilled.

खीर

khīr

Shopping

Shopping in Indian markets can be a lot of fun. You will find excellent prices on silver jewelry, cotton dyed bedsheets, cloth, and regional handicrafts, just to name a few items. Be prepared to bargain with the shopkeeper. Bargaining is part of the art of shopping at the market. If you do not like the final price you are given, feel free to walk away. In larger stores or shops prices can be fixed. In such stores you might see a sign that says एक दाम (*ek dām*) or "one price."

While most shopkeepers are just trying to make an honest living, unfortunately some might try to take advantage of you because you are a tourist. If you are in the market for silk, for example, you might want to find out beforehand what the going rate is from people at your hotel, etc. Do not expect to pay the same price that a local would pay, however. In many cities you can shop at government-run emporiums that have reasonable, fixed prices on all goods.

Taxi and auto-rickshaw drivers will sometimes want to take you to a shop on the way to your destination because they receive a commission from the shopkeeper. If you are not interested in going there, insist that the driver not stop. You also might be approached by people trying to sell you things such as chess sets and marble boxes. Be careful about people who ask you to go back to their shop with them. Although many of these salespeople are legitimate, unfortunately some tourists have become involved in precarious situations. While in major cities, use your best judgment as you would in large American cities.

Where can I buy. . . ?
. . . कहाँ मिलेगा ।
. . . kahāN milegā?

Note: This literally means "where is . . . available?"

Do you have silk saris?
रेशमी साड़ियाँ आप के पास हैं ।
reśamī sāṛiyāN āp ke pās haiN?

What kind of sari is this?
यह कैसी साड़ी है ।
yeh kaisī sāṛī hai?

I need some [red] cloth.
मुझे कुछ [लाल] कपड़ा चाहिये ।
mujhe kuch [lāl] kapṛā cāhiye.

I want to have a shirt made.
मैं क़मीज़ बनवाना चाहता *m.* / चाहती *f.* हूँ ।
maiN kamīz banvānā cāhatā *m.* / cāhatī *f.* hūN.

How much is this one?
यह वाला कितने का है ।
yeh wālā kitne ka hai?

That is too expensive. I'll give you . . . rupees for it.
यह बहुत ही महँगा है . . . रुपये दूँगा *m.* / दूँगी *f.* ।
yeh bahut hi maheNgā hai. . . . rupaye dūNgā *m.* / dūNgī *f.*

I am only looking.
मैं सिर्फ़ देख रहा *m.* / रही *f.* हूँ ।
maiN sirf dekh rahā *m.* / rahī *f.* hūN.

I'll come back tomorrow.
कल वापस आऊँगा *m.* / आऊँगी *f.* ।
kal vāpas āūNgā *m.* / āūNgī *f.*

OK, then I'll take it.
ठीक है तब ले लूँगा *m.* / लूँगी *f.* ।
ṭhīk hai tab le lūNgā *m.* / lūNgī *f.*

Do you have any others?
आप के पास कोई और हैं ।
āp ke pās koī aur haiN?

I don't like these. Please show me more.
मुझे ये पसंद नहीं हैं । ज़रा और दिखाइये ।
mujhe ye pasand nahīN haiN. zarā aur dikhāiye.

This is very beautiful, isn't it?
यह बहुत सुनदर है, ना ।
yeh bahut sundar hai, nā?

Thank you. See you later. Goodbye.
शुक्रिया । फिर मिलेंगे । नमस्ते - जी ।
śukriyā. phir mileNge. namaste jī.

Note: Here by adding the suffix *jī* you are already showing respect. There is no need to use the more formal *namaskār* when you are paying for services. Indians often feel that Americans say "thank you" too much. For instance, in a restaurant, thanking an Indian waiter every time he comes over to refill your water glass might make him feel awkward. He will most likely feel compelled to say "thank you" back to you. This may be partly due to the fact that in Hindi there is no word for "you're welcome." Instead, people say "don't mention it" or "it was nothing." Also, between friends saying "thank you" for small things will often seem too formal in India. People show their appreciation by expressing their pleasure and doing favors in return.

bookstore
किताब की दुकान
kitāb kī dukān

clothing store
कपड़े की दुकान
kapṛe kī dukān

shoe store
जूते की दुकान
jūte kī dukān

sweet shop
मिठाई की दुकान
miṭhāī kī dukān

tailor
दर्ज़ी
darzī

vegetable seller
सब्ज़ी वाला
sabzī wālā

Services

Barber

Please give me a haircut.
बाल काट दीजिये ।
bāl kaṭ dījiye.

Please don't cut my hair too short.
बहुत छोटा न काटियेगा ।
bahut choṭā na kāṭiyegā.

I need a shave.
मुझे दाढ़ी बनवाना है ।
mujhe dāḍhī banvānā hai.

Note: Getting a shave at an Indian barber shop can be quite enjoyable as the price usually includes a head massage.

Phone, Fax & Internet

I want to call the United States.
मुझे अमेरिका फ़ोन करना है ।
mujhe americā fon karnā hai.

How much is one minute?
एक मिनट के लिये कितने पैसे लगते हैं ।
ek minaṭ ke liye kitne paise lagte haiN?

The line is busy.
लाइन व्यस्त है ।
lāin vyast hai.

All lines are busy.
सभी लाइनें व्यस्त हैं ।
sabhī lāine vyast haiN.

I've been disconnected.
लाइन कट गयी ।
lāin kaṭ gayī.

I need to call this number.
मुझे इस नंबर पर फ़ोन करना है ।
mujhe is nambar par fone karnā hai.

Do you have any faxes for me?
क्या मेरे लिये कोई फ़ैक्स आया है ।
kyā mere liye koī faiks āya hai?

Where can I go to send a fax?
फ़ैक्स कहाँ भेज सकता *m.* / सकती *f.* हूँ ।
faiks kahāN bhej saktā *m.* / saktī *f.* hūN?

What is your telephone / fax number?
आप का फ़ोन / फ़ैक्स नमबर क्या है ।
āp kā fon / faiks namber kyā hai?

Where can I go to use the Internet?
इन्टरनेट कहाँ इस्तेमाल कर सकूँ ।
internet kahāN istemāl kar sakūN?

I would like to send e-mail.
ई - मेल भेजना चाहता *m.* / चाहती *f.* हूँ ।
e-mail bhejnā cāhatā *m.* / cāhatī *f.* hūN.

Bank / Money Exchange

The basic unit of Indian currency is the rupee (Rs.) It is best for travelers to exchange traveler's checks or dollars at a bank. You can exchange American Express traveler's checks at any American Express office in India with no commission. Many Indian banks also offer credit card cash advances. In major cities you now will find ATM machines. As you spend time in India you will undoubtedly be approached to have money changed on the "black market." Although the exchange rate is quite favorable, it is not recommended for reasons of safety. Moreover, it is not legal. Be sure to save all of your exchange receipts in case you need to show them to change your rupees back into dollars before departing from India.

Where can I exchange money?
पैसे कहाँ बदल सकता *m.* / सकती *f.* हूँ ।
paise kahāN badal saktā *m.* / saktī *f.* hūN?

Can I exchange U.S. dollars here?
क्या मैं यहाँ डॉलर बदल सकता *m.* / सकती *f.* हूँ ।
kyā maiN yahāN ḍālar badal saktā *m.* /
saktī *f.* hūN?

Can I exchange traveler's checks here?
क्या मैं यहाँ ट्रेवलर्स चेक बदल सकता *m.* / सकती *f.* हूँ ।
kyā maiN yahāN ṭrevalars cek badal saktā *m.* / saktī *f.* hūN?

What is today's exchange rate?
आज का एक्सचेंग रेट क्या है ।
āj kā eksceng reṭ kyā hai?

Can I take a [Visa Card] cash advance here?
यहाँ [वीज़ा कार्ड] पर पैसे निकाल सकता *m.* / सकती *f.* हूँ ।
yahāN [vīsā kārḍ] par paise nikāl saktā *m.* / saktī *f.* hūN?

Tobacco

Please give me one package of (name of brand) cigarettes.
मुझे एक पैकेट . . . दीजिये ।
mujhe ek paikeṭ . . . dījiye.

Is it OK to smoke here?
क्या यहाँ सिगरेट पीना ठीक है ।
kyā yahāN sigreṭ pīnā ṭhīk hai?

Laundry

I need to have these clothes cleaned (washed).
मुझे ये कपड़े साफ़ करवाने हैं ।
mujhe ye kapṛe sāf karvāne haiN.

I need this [shirt] pressed.
मुझे यह [क़मीज़] प्रेस करवाना है ।
mujhe yeh [kamīz] pres karvānā hai.

When will you return?
आप कब वापस आयेंगे ।
āp kab vāpas āyeNge?

How long will it take?
कितना समय लगेगा ।
kitnā samay lagegā?

Religion & Worship

You will want to consult a detailed guidebook if you are planning to visit a temple or mosque, as restrictions vary. You will need to take off your shoes before entering most temples. Many temples have separate areas for men and women. In a Sikh temple your head must be covered at all times. Mosques have various restrictions on dress and admittance. Visiting religious sites in India is extremely important as it will give you insight into the diverse religious traditions of the Indian Subcontinent. You will appreciate your visit even more if you read about the history and background of various religious sites before you go. If you are at an active temple, please be respectful when taking photos.

We want to go to a . . .
हम. . . जाना चाहते हैं ।
ham . . . jānā cāhate haiN.

> **church.**
> गिरजाघर (or) चर्च
> girjāghar (or) carc
>
> **Hindu temple.**
> मंदिर
> mandir

mosque.
मस्जिद
masjid

Sikh temple.
गुरूद्वारा
gurudvārā

Jain temple.
जैन मंदिर
jain mandir

Jewish synagogue.
यहूदियों का मंदिर
yahūdiyoN kā mandir

Are we allowed to go inside here?
क्या हम अंदर जा सकते हैं ।
kyā ham andar jā sakte haiN?

Is photography allowed inside?
क्या अंदर फ़ोटोग्रफ़ी कर सकते हैं ।
kyā andar fotografī kar sakte haiN?

Is my clothing appropriate for this temple?
इस मंदिर में जाने के लिये क्या मेरे कपड़े ठीक है ।
is mandir meN jāne ke liye kyā mere kapṛe ṭhīk hai?

Are non-Hindus allowed in here?
क्या वे लोग अंदर जा सकते जो हिंदू नहीं हैं ।
kyā ve log andar jā sakte jo hindū nahīN haiN?

Please take off your shoes before entering.
कृपया अपने जूते यहाँ उतारिये ।
kripya apne jūte yahāN utāriye.

I am . . .
मैं. . . हूँ ।
maiN . . . hūN.

Muslim.
मुसलमान
musalmān

Hindu.
हिन्दू
hindū

Jewish.
यहूदी
yahūdī

Sikh.
सिख
sikh

Christian.
ईसाई
īsāī

Sightseeing & Entertainment

What time does this place open?
यह जगह कितने बजे खुलती है ।
yeh jagah kitne baje khultī hai?

What time does this place close?
यह जगह कितने बजे बंद होती है ।
yeh jagah kitne baje band hotī hai?

It is closed on [Mondays].
[सोमवार] को बंद रहती है ।
[somvār] ko band rehtī hai.

We need a guide.
हम को गाइड चाहिये ।
ham ko gāiḍ cāhiye.

We don't need a guide.
हम को गाइड नहीं चाहिये ।
ham ko gāiḍ nahīN cāhiye.

Do you have a map of Delhi?
आप के पास दिल्ली का नक़्शा है ।
āp ke pās dillī kā naqśā hai?

May I take a photo of you?
ज़रा मैं आप की तस्वीर खींच लूँ ।
zarā maiN āp kī tasvīr khiNc lūN?

Which building is this?
यह कौनसी इमारत है ।
yeh kaunsī imārat hai?

I want to see a Hindi film.
मैं हिन्दी फ़िल्म देखना चाहता *m.* / चाहती *f.* हूँ ।
maiN hindī film dekhnā cāhatā *m.* /
cāhatī *f.* hūN.

Note: Experience "Bollywood" for yourself! Most Indians go to the cinema and their passion for films and film stars transcends all social classes. Although you may not understand much of the dialogue, most of the plots are universal in nature and often involve themes of love, marriage, family, etc. Most of all you will enjoy the numerous song and dance numbers in most Hindi films. If you enjoy Hindi film music you can go to any music shop and purchase cassettes and CDs of film soundtracks. You will often hear the most popular songs being played in the streets and in markets day and night.

Where is the cinema?
सिनेमा कहाँ है ।
sinemā kahāN hai?

Can you recommend a good Hindi film?
क्या आप अच्छी हिन्दी फ़िल्म की सिफ़ारिश कर सकते हैं ।
kyā āp acchī hindī film kī sifāriś kar sakte
haiN?

Who is your favorite actor / actress?
आप का मनपसंद अभिनेता / अभिनेत्री कौन है ।
āp kā manpasand abhinetā / abhinetrī kaun hai?

Problems & Difficult Situations

Use your best judgment while traveling in India as you would in the U.S. and Europe, especially at night in major cities. For the most part it is not safe for women to walk alone late at night. Keep your valuables hidden in a money belt or pouch that is not easily accessible. In general, India is a very safe country. For more information please refer to the Cultural Notes section.

Please help me!
मदद करें ।
madad kareN!

Please leave me / us alone.
हमको अकेला छोड़ दें ।
hamko akelā coṛ deN.

Don't do that.
ऐसा मत करो ।
esā mat karo.

Don't touch me!
हाथ मत लगाओ ।
hāth mat lagāo!

Stop! Thief!
रुको ।चोर ।
ruko! cor!

My . . . has been stolen.
मेरे. . . की चोरी हो गयी है ।
mere . . . kī corī ho gayī hai.

bag
थैला
thailā

luggage
सामान
sāmān

money
पैसा
paisā

airline tickets
एयर टिकट
eyar ṭikaṭ

camera
कैमरा
kaimarā

passport
पॉसपोर्ट
pāsporṭ

I was attacked.
किसी ने मुझपर हमला किया है ।
kisī ne mujhpar hamlā kiyā hai.

I don't want any marijuana. Please leave me alone.
मुझे गंजा नहीं चाहिये । मुझे छोड़िये ।
mujhe ganjā nahīN cāhiye. mujhe choṛiye.

Please take me to the U.S. Embassy.
अमेरिकन दूतावास को ले जाइये ।
amerikan dūtāvās ko le jāiye.

I am about to call the police.
मैं पुलिस को फोन करने वाला *m.* / वाली *f.* हूँ ।
maiN pulis ko fone karne wālā *m.* / wālī *f.* hūN.

Is this area safe?
क्या यह जगह सुरक्षित है ।
kyā yeh jagah surakṣit hai?

Where is the nearest police station?
सबसे नज़दीक पुलीस थाना कहाँ है ।
sabse nazdīk pulīs thānā kahāN hai?

I am sorry.
माफ़ कीजिये
māf kījiye

Absolutely not.
बिलकुल नहीं ।
bilkul nahīN.

I don't want to offend you.
बुरा मत मानिये ।
burā mat māniye.

I need your help.
मुझे आप की मदद चाहिये ।
mujhe āp kī madad cāhiye.

Somebody get the police!
कोई जल्दी पुलिस को बुलाओ ।
koī jaldī pulis ko bulāo!

Somebody call a doctor!
कोई जल्दी एक डॉकटर को बुलाओ ।
koī jaldī ek ḍākṭar ko bulāo!

This isn't your fault.
आप की ग़लती नहीं है ।
āp kī qgaltī nahīN hai.

This isn't my fault.
मेरी ग़लती नहीं है ।
merī qgaltī nahīN hai.

This is a huge problem.
बहुत बड़ी समस्या है ।
bahut baṛī samasyā hai.

You are very kind.
आप की बड़ी कृपा है ।
āp kī baṛī kripa hai.

I am very thankful for your help.

आप की मदद के लिये बहुत धन्यवाद देता *m.* / देती *f.* हूँ ।

āp kī madad ke liye bahut dhanyavād detā *m.* / detī *f.* hūN.

There has been an accident.

दुर्घटना हो गई है ।

dūrghaṭnā ho gaī hai.

My friend is hurt.

मेरा दोस्त को चोट लग गई है ।

merā dost ko coṭ lag gaī hai.

Health & Wellness

You will want to take every precaution to stay healthy while traveling in India. Most travelers become ill from not being careful about water. Only drink bottled water that comes to you with its seal intact. Avoid ice in drinks as well as juice from fresh-squeezed juice stands. You should bring all of your required medications with you as well as any favorite brands of stomach-upset medicine, painkillers, etc. Items such as condoms and tampons should be brought from home as the quality and availability of these cannot be guaranteed in India. If you need to buy medicine, you can find almost any type that you would need at any pharmacy (chemist).

I am sick.
मैं बीमार हूँ ।
maiN bīmār hūN.

I have insurance.
बीमा है ।
bīmā hai.

My friend is [very] ill.
मेरा दोस्त [बहुत] बीमार है ।
merā dost [bahut] bīmār hai.

Is there a doctor who speaks English?
कोई ड़ॉक्तर है जिन को अंग्रेज़ी आती है ।
koī ḍāktar hai jinko aNgrezī ātī hai?

I have a headache.
मेरा सिर दूख रहा है ।
merā sir dūkh rahā hai.

I need painkillers.
मुझे दर्द की दवा चाहिये ।
mujhe dard kī davā cāhiye.

I am pregnant.
मैंा गर्भवती हूँ ।
maiN garabhvatī hūN.

I might be pregnant.
हो सकता है कि मैं गर्भवती हूँ ।
ho saktā hai ki maiN garabhvatī hūN.

I might have a venereal disease.
हो सकता है कि गुप्त रोग है ।
ho saktā hai ki gupt rog hai.

I am diabetic.
मैं मधुमेही हूँ ।
maiN madhumehī hūN.

I need medicine for . . .
मुझ . . . के लिये दवा चाहिये ।
mujhe . . . ke liye davā cāhiye.

nausea.
मिचली
miclī

sore throat.
गले में दर्द
gale meN dard

fever.
बुख़ार
buqhār

rash.
ददोरा
dadorā

diarrhea.
दस्त
dast

constipation.
क़ब्ज़
qabz

toothache.
दाँत मे दर्द
dāNt meN dard

I am allergic to. . . .
मुझे . . . से एलरगी है ।
mujhe . . . se elargī hai.

I take this medication.
मैं यह दवा लेता *m.* / लेती *f.* / हूँ ।
maiN yeh davā letā *m.* / letī *f.* hūN.

What kind of antibiotics do you have?
आप के पास किस प्रकार की ऐंटीबायटिक हैं ।
āp ke pās kis prakar kī ainṭībāyaṭik haiN?

I was bitten by a . . .
मुझे . . . ने काटा है ।
mujhe . . . ne kāṭā hai.

monkey.
बन्दर
bandar

dog.
कुत्ता
kuttā

snake.
साँप
sāNp

I am dehydrated.
मेरे अंदर का पानी सूख गया है ।
mere andar kā pānī sūkh gayā hai.

Please give me a packet of Electrol (rehydration salts).
एक पॅकेट एलेक्ट्रोल दे दीजिये ।
ek paket̩ Elekt̩rol de dījiye.

Please write it down.
ज़रा लिख दीजिये ।
zarā likh dījiye.

How many times per day?
एक दिन में कितनी बार ।
ek din meN kitnī bār?

Take one pill every day.
दिन में एक गोली एक बार ।
din meN ek golī ek bār.

For how many days?
कितने दिनों के लिये ।
kitne dinoN ke liye?

before eating
खाने से पहले
khāne se pehale

at meals
खाने के समय
khāne ke samay

after eating
खाने के बाद
khāne ke bād

I need to see a gynecologist.
मैं औरतों की डॉक्टर से मिलना चाहती हूँ।
maiN aurtoN kī ḍākṭar se milnā cāhatī hūN.

I have menstrual pain.
मुझे मासिक का दर्द हो रहा है।
mujhe māsik kā dard ho rahā hai.

My period is late.
मुझे मासिक में देर हो गई है।
mujhe māsik meN der ho gaī hai.

I would like to see an Ayurvedic (traditional Indian medicine) doctor.
मैं आयुर्वेदिक वैद्य से मिलना चाहता *m.* / चाहती *f.* हूँ।
maiN āyurvaidik vaidya se milnā cāhatā *m.* / cāhatī *f.* hūN.

I would like to see a dentist.
मैं डेंटिस्ट से मिलना चाहता *m.* / चाहती *f.* हूँ।
maiN ḍenṭisṭ se milnā cāhatā *m.* / cāhatī *f.* hūN.

I have pain here.
यहाँ दर्द हो रहा है।
yahāN dard ho rahā hai.

I have pain in my. . . .
मुझे. . . में दर्द है।
mujhe . . . meN dard hai.

My arm is broken.
बाज़ू टूटा है ।
bāzū ṭūṭā hai.

Parts of the Body

arm
बाज़ू
bāzū

back
पीठ
pīṭh

body
शरीर
śarīr

bone
हड्डी
haḍḍī

chest
छाती
chātī

ear
कान
kān

eye
आँख
āNkh

face
मुँह
muNh

finger
उँगली
uNgalī

foot
पैर
pair

hair
बाल
bāl

hand
हाथ
hāth

head
सिर
sir

kidney
गुर्दा
gurdā

knee
घुटना
ghuṭnā

leg
टाँग
ṭāNg

liver
कलेजा
kalejā

lungs
फेफड़ा
phephṛā

neck
गरदन
gardan

nose
नाक
nāk

stomach
पेट
peṭ

tooth
दाँत
dāNt

How do you feel?
आप की तबीयत कैसी है ।
āp kī tabīyat kaisī hai?

I feel weak.
मुझे कमज़ोरी लग रही है ।
mujhe kamzorī lag rahī hai.

I feel dizzy.
मुझे चक्कर आ रहे हैं ।
mujhe cakkar ā rahe haiN.

I feel better than before.
पहले से तबीयात ठीक है ।
pehale se tabīyāt ṭhīk hai.

I'm all better.
एकदम फ़िट हो गया *m.* / गई *f.* हूँ ।
ekdam fiṭ ho gayā *m.* / gaī *f.* hūN.

Other Health Words

asthmatic
दमा रोगी
damā rogī

blood
खून
qhūn

blood pressure
रक्तचाप
raktacāp

cold
जुकाम
zukām

cough
खाँसी
khāNsī

dentist
डेंटिस्ट
ḍenṭisṭ

drugs (medicine)
दवाई
davāī

drugs (illegal, *lit.* "intoxicating")
नशीला दवाई
naśīlā davāī

Idioms & Expressions

What will be will be seen (i.e., "whatever is meant to be will be.")
जो होना है सो देखा जायेगा ।
jo honā hai so dekhā jāyegā.

Will that work OK for you?
चलेगा ।
calegā?

God bless you!
भगवान भला करे ।
bhagavān bhalā kare!

It's in God's hands.
ऊपरवाले के हाथ में है ।
ūparvāle ke hāth meN hai.

Everyone's God is One. (This is a famous phrase of the Indian saint Shirdi Sai Baba, who promoted the oneness of all religion.)
सब का मालिक एक ।
sab kā mālik ek.

Nonsense!
बकवास ।
bakvās!

to be extremely embarassed (*lit.* to drown in a handful of water)
चुल्लू भर पानी में डूब मरना
cullū bhar pānī meN ḍūb marnā

By your blessings . . .
आप के आशीर्वाद से. . .
āp ke āśīrvād se . . .

Shall we get going?
अब हम चलें ।
ab ham cheleN?

What happened?
क्या हुआ ।
kyā huā?

There is no benefit in this (there's no point in doing this).
इस में कोई फ़ायदा नहीं है ।
is meN koī faidā nahīN hai.

I am very happy to hear about this.
यह बात सुन कर मुझे बहुत ही खुशी हुई ।
yeh bāt sun kar mujhe bahut hī khuśī huī.

Wow!
अरे वाह ।
are wah!

That's amazing (said when impressed or moved by something such as music or poetry).
क्या बात है ।
kyā bāt hai.

It is very auspicious (favorable and fortunate).
बहुत शुभ है ।
bahut śubh hai.

Unbelieveable!
विश्वास नहीं होता ।
viśvās nahīN hotā!

Heed what I say!
मेरी बात मानो ।
merī bāt māno!

I don't care about. . . .
मुझे. . . की परवाह नहीं है ।
mujhe . . . kī parvāh nahīN hai.

When in Rome, do as the Romans do. (This phrase can be used when people remark how pleased they are that you are wearing Indian clothing, speaking Hindi, or taking an interest in something Indian. It is sure to bring a smile every time.)
जैसा देश वैसा वेश ।
jaisā deś vaisā veś.

Great! (also "cool" and "neat")
बढ़िया ।
baṛhiyā!

I can't even express how wonderful this is.
इतना बढ़िया की हम बता नहीं सकते हैं ।
itnā baṛhiyā kī ham batā nahīN sakte haiN.

Well done!
शाबाश ।
śābāś!

Weather

What beautiful weather!
क्या सुहाना मौसम है ।
kyā suhānā mausam hai!

It's raining.
बारिश हो रही है ।
bāriś ho rahī hai.

It's very foggy.
कुहरा बहुत है ।
kuharā bahut hai.

It's very sunny.
धूप बहुत तेज़ है ।
dhūp bahut tez hai.

It's very windy.
तेज़ हवा चल रही है ।
tez havā cal rahī hai.

It's [very] cold.
[बहुत] ठण्डा है ।
[bahut] ṭhaṇḍā hai.

It's so hot today.
बहुत गर्मी है आज ।
bahut garmī hai āj.

It's very humid.
बहुत उमस है ।
bahut umas hai.

It has gotten dark.
अंधेरा हो गया है ।
aNdherā ho gayā hai.

What is the temperature today?
आज का तापमान कितना है ।
āj kā tāpmān kitnā hai?

Is it going to rain tomorrow?
क्या कल बारिश होगी ।
kyā kal bāriś hogī?

A big storm is coming.
बड़ा तूफ़ान आ रहा है ।
baṛā tūfān ā rahā hai.

Temperature Conversion

To convert temperatures from ***Celsius*** to Fahrenheit, multiply the Celsius temperature by 9/5, then add 32.

To convert from ***Fahrenheit*** to Celsius, subtract 32 and multiply by 5/9.

Time, Days & Seasons

The following examples show patterns of how to express time. You can follow these patterns for most hours of the day, except for the hours of one and two (both A.M. and P.M.), which are treated differently as shown below. When telling time in Hindi, it is best to think in terms of "quarter after" and "quarter to" instead of 1:15, 1:45, etc. This will help you to remember the word order and to choose the correct hour in your phrase.

You can use this format for the hours of three to twelve:

It is [three] o'clock.
[तीन] बजे हैं ।
[tīn] baje haiN.

It is quarter past [three].
सवा [तीन] बजे हैं ।
savā [tīn] baje haiN.

It is [three]-thirty.
साढ़े [तीन] बजे हैं ।
sāṛhe [tīn] baje haiN.

It is quarter to [three].
पौने [तीन] बजे हैं ।
paune [tīn] baje haiN.

Use this format for the hours of one and two:

It is one o'clock.
एक बजा है ।
ek bajā hai.

It is quarter past one.
सवा एक बजा है ।
savā ek bajā hai.

It is 1:30.
डेढ़ बजा है ।
ḍeḍh (pronounced more like "dare") bajā hai.

It is quarter to one (12:45).
पौन बजा है ।
paun bajā hai.

It is two o'clock.
दो बजे हैं ।
do baje haiN.

It is 2:30.
ढाई बजे हैं ।
ḍhāī baje haiN.

It is quarter to two (1:45).
पौने दो बजे हैं ।
paune do baje haiN.

morning
सुबह
subah

noon
दोपहर
dopahar

afternoon
बाद दोपहर
bād dopahar

evening
शाम
śām

night
रात
rāt

yesterday morning
कल सुबह
kal subah

tomorrow evening
कल शाम
kal śām

hour
घंटा
ghanṭā

minute
मिनट
minaṭ

second
सेकेन्ड
sekenḍ

Days of the Week

Monday
सोमवार
somvār

Tuesday
मंगलवार
mangalvār

Wednesday
बुधवार
budhvār

Thursday
गुरुवार
guruvār

Friday
शुक्रवार
śukravār

Saturday
शनिवार
śanivār

Sunday
रविवार
ravivār

Seasons

Spring
वसंत
vasant

Summer
गर्मी
garmī

Winter (or cold season)
जाड़ा
jāṛā

Rainy Season
बरसात
barsāt

day
दिन
din

week
हफ़्ता
haftā

month
महीना
mahīnā

year
साल
sāl

this [week]
इस [हफ़्ते]
is [hafte]

next [week]
अगले [हफ़्ते]
agle [hafte]

today
आज
āj

yesterday / tomorrow
कल
kal

day after tomorrow / day before yesterday
परसों
parsoN

See you tomorrow!
कल मिलेंगे ।
kal mileNge!

next time
अगली बार
aglī bār

[two] times
[दो] बार
[do] bār

last time
पिछली बार
pichlī bār

I will go back to America [tomorrow evening].
[कल शाम] को अमेरिका वापस जाऊँगा *m.* / जाऊँगी *f.* ।
[kal śām] ko amerikā vāpas jāūNgā *m.* / jāūNgī *f.*

Months

January
जनवरी
janvarī

February
फ़रवरी
farvarī

March
मार्च
mārc

April
अप्रैल
aprail

May
मई
maī

June
जून
jūn

July
जुलाई
julāī

August
अगस्त
agast

September
सितम्बर
sitambar

October
अक्तूबर
aktūbar

November
नवम्बर
navambar

December
दिसम्बर
disambar

Note: The above months correspond to the Western calendar, which is used by most of the business world in India. However, you should know that the traditional Hindu calendar runs 57 years ahead of the Western calendar and has different names for the months. Also, the Islamic calendar began in the year 622 when Muhammad left Mecca. Both the Hindu and Islamic calendars play a vibrant and important role in the lives of Hindus and Muslims.

Religious Holidays

Below is a list of major religious holidays in India. Please be aware that these are just basic descriptions and the way in which these festivals are celebrated often varies by region.

Shivaratri (Feb. / Mar.): On this day Hindus fast and perform special acts of worship *(puja)* in honor of Lord Shiva, who dances his cosmic dance, simultaneously destroying and recreating the universe.

Holi (Feb. / Mar.): Celebrated to mark the end of winter, this is a time when Hindus throw colored dyes on each other and set off firecrackers. In recent times, unfortunately, some people throw metalic silver paint instead of the traditional *gulāl* powder dyes. Depending upon where you are, this festival could get out of hand as many people feel that it is a day to let go of all inhibitions. Women travelers should be especially careful. If you go out you most likely will get hit with colored dye, so do not wear your good clothes on this day.

Raksha Bandhan (Jul. / Aug.): On this Hindu holiday, sisters tie sacred threads known as *rakhis* to the wrists of their brothers (or those whom they consider to be as brothers) for protection. In return, brothers give their sisters gifts.

Ganesh Chaturthi (Aug. / Sept.): This Hindu festival honors the birth of Lord Ganesh, the elephant-headed God who helps devotees overcome all obstacles. Images of Lord Ganesh are paraded through the streets and eventually immersed in the Ganges or another body of water.

Janmashthami (Aug. / Sept.): On this day Hindus celebrate the birth of Krishna with joy and mischief. The festivities are especially elaborate in Mathura, the birthplace of Lord Krishna.

Dushera (Sept. / Oct.): This festival marks the triumph of good (Lord Rama) over evil (Rama's brother Ravana). Large effigies of Ravana are burned and immersed in the river. Many Hindus also perform *puja* for the goddess Durga on this day.

Diwali (Oct. / Nov.): This Hindu festival of lights lasts for many days and is celebrated with great joy throughout the country. Hindus clean their houses, wear new clothing and light oil lamps to guide Lord Rama home from his exile in Sri Lanka. Sweets are often exchanged and firecrackers set off. In holy centers such as Varanasi, lamps cover the banks of the river, creating a beautiful display.

Nanak Jayanti (Nov. / Dec.): On this day Sikhs celebrate the birth of their religion's founder, Guru Nanak.

Ramadan (varies): This is a thirty-day fasting period for Muslims. It falls at different times of year on the Western calendar, due to the lunar nature of the Islamic calendar. Ramadan corresponds to the time when the Prophet Muhammad received the revelation of the Qur'an in the holy city of Mecca.

Eid al-Fitr (varies): This day marks the end of Ramadan and is celebrated by Muslims with feasting.

Numbers

The following list shows the pronunciation of numbers in Hindi. Unlike in many other languages, there is no clear-cut pattern to this. Numbers in Hindi are written like this:

०	१	२	३	४	५	६	७	८	९
0	1	2	3	4	5	6	7	8	9

1 ek
2 do
3 tīn
4 cār
5 pāNc
6 chah (more like che)
7 sāt
8 āṭh
9 nau
10 das
11 gyārah
12 bārah
13 terah
14 caudah
15 pandrah
16 solah
17 satrah
18 aṭhārah
19 unnīs
20 bīs
21 ikkīs

22 bāīs
23 teīs
24 caubīs
25 paccīs
26 chabbīs
27 satāīs
28 aṭṭhāīs
29 untīs
30 tīs
31 iktīs
32 battīs
33 taiNtīs
34 cauNtīs
35 paiNtīs
36 chatīs
37 saiNtīs
38 aṛtīs
39 untālīs
40 cālīs
41 iktālīs
42 bayālīs
43 taiNtālīs
44 cavālīs
45 paiNtālīs
46 chiyālīs
47 saiNtālīs
48 aṛtālīs
49 uncās
50 pacās
51 ikyāvan
52 bāvan

53 tirpan
54 cauvan
55 pacpan
56 chappan
57 satāvan
58 aṭṭhāvan
59 unsaṭh
60 sāṭh
61 iksaṭh
62 bāsaṭh
63 tirsaṭh
64 cauNsaṭh
65 paiNsaṭh
66 chiyāsaṭh
67 sarsaṭh
68 aṛsaṭh
69 unhattar
70 sattar
71 ikhattar
72 bahattar
73 tihattar
74 cauhattar
75 pachattar
76 chihattar
77 satattar
78 aṭhhattar
79 unyāsī
80 assī
81 ikyāsī
82 bayāsī
83 tirāsī

84 caurāsī
85 pacāsī
86 chiyāsī
87 sattāsī
88 aṭṭhāsī
89 navāsī
90 nabbe
91 ikyānve
92 bānve
93 tirānve
94 caurānve
95 pacānve
96 chyānve
97 sattānve
98 aṭṭhānve
99 ninyānve
100 sau

101
एक सौ एक
ek sau ek

208
दो सौ आठ
do sau āṭh

1000
एक हज़ार
ek hazār

100,000
एक लाख
ek lākh

10,000,000
एक करोड़
ek karoṛ (crore)

[50] percent
पचास प्रतिशत
[pacās] pratiśat

thousands of people
हज़ारों लोग
hazāroN log

first
पहला
pehalā

second
दूसरा
dūsrā

third
तीसरा
tīsrā

fourth
चौथा
cauthā

fifth
पाँचवाँ
pāNcvāN

sixth
छठा
chaṭhā

seventh
सातवाँ
sātvāN

eighth
आठवाँ
āṭhvāN

ninth
नवाँ
navāN

tenth
दसवाँ
dasvāN

Cultural Notes

These are things to keep in mind so that you will not offend Indians and so they will not offend you:

- Wearing shorts or other skimpy clothing is very offensive to most Indians. While there are certain places where this is tolerated, such as in the beach areas of Goa or in Mumbai, generally it is best to dress a little more conservatively (no shorts or sleeveless shirts), especially for women. You will see students and young people in India wearing jeans and t-shirts. However, for the most part shorts are not worn by Indians out in public. You can have Indian clothes tailor-made for you very cheaply. This type of clothing is also more appropriate for the climate. For every rule in India there are exceptions, so use your best judgment and watch and learn from your surroundings.

- Taking photographs of people without asking permission is offensive. If you wish to take someone's photo, please ask first.

- When entering a temple, please observe the regulations. In most Hindu temples you will need to take your shoes off. In a

Sikh temple, you will need to have your head covered. If you are unsure, talk to someone at your hotel beforehand.

- Please do not take photographs at the cremation grounds in Varanasi (or elsewhere). This is extremely offensive.

- Giving money to beggars is not advised as a general rule. Please use your common sense. In many cases money given to street beggars is taken away by a "ringleader," so to speak. If you wish, you can help people the most by offering to buy food for them. That is not to say that you should never give. Just use your best judgment and realize that as soon as you give to one person, you will attract attention from many more people.

- The term *baqhśīś* can mean "tip" or "gratuity," but usually it refers to money paid beforehand. In some cases this could be considered a "bribe." If you are in a very difficult situation and need something done, offering a little money might be appropriate. An example of this would be if you were stranded at a train station at 2 A.M. and told that there were no more seats available. Be careful and evaluate each situation. While giving "bribes" is not something to encourage, *baqhśīś* is a part of Indian culture and the traveler should be aware of this.

- Women traveling alone should take extra precautions in certain situations. When traveling by train, book a seat in the "women's car," which has a security guard and is for women only. Do not walk around urban areas late at night by yourself.

- Many Westerners are offended when some Indians stare at them. While it is rude to stare in the U.S., Indians are usually doing this out of interest and do not mean to be rude. Indians also might ask very direct questions about your salary or the cost of items you have brought with you from home. This is out of mere curiousity and is not meant to be rude.

- You might observe men in certain places using the street as their "restroom" on occasion. In a country of one billion people, it is not always practical to find a public restroom.

- Since the left hand is used by most Indians to clean themselves with water after using the restroom, it is generally considered rude to eat with the left hand. You can handle food with both hands, but the hand that passes the food to your mouth should be your right hand.

- Do not get angry with people for trying to overcharge you for things. There are many people in India who work for a month or more to earn what we might earn in one day. Most people are aware of the favorable exchange rate, which adds to this practice. This does not mean that you should pay more for things. Just be aware of this.

- Public display of affection between members of the opposite sex is not common in most of India. Members of the same sex, especially men, will be seen holding hands while standing and walking in public as a sign of friendship.

- Enjoy yourself, be curious, and talk with people. Since you are learning Hindi, many Indians will be thrilled to help you practice. The above points have been mentioned because they are very common problems and misconceptions that you can become aware of so that they do not interfere with your experience. While there are many stereotypes about Indians, there are also many stereotypes about foreigners in

India. For example, many Indians think that Western women are "easy," so to speak, due to the way they are portrayed in films. Also, many Indians assume that if you have enough money to travel to India then you must live in a huge home and drive an expensive car. Remember that you are a representative of your own country and culture while in India. Please take a respectful attitude toward Indians and you will receive the same treatment in return.

Other Regional Interest Titles from Hippocrene Books

CUISINE

The Indian Spice Kitchen
Expanded Edition
Monisha Bharadwaj

This cookbook takes readers on an unforgettable culinary journey along the spice routes of India with over 200 recipes. Color photographs appear throughout. Simple recipes, adapted for the North American kitchen, allow the home chef to create delicious foods with precious saffron, aromatic tamarind, and delicately fragrant tumeric, mustard, and chilies. The recipes are arranged by a featured ingredient in a full range of soups, breads, vegetarian and meat dishes, as well as beverages and desserts. Historical and cultural information are provided for each ingredient. Also included are facts on storage and preparation, medicinal and ritual uses, as well as cooking times and serving suggestions for all recipes. Color photographs are featured throughout.

Full-Color • 240 pages • 10¼ x 8 • $29.50hc • 0-7818-1143-0 • W • (16)

Flavorful India
Treasured Recipes from a Gujarati Family
Priti Chitnis Gress

The cuisine of the Western Indian state of Gujarat is famed for its delicately flavored vegetarian dishes. Hot, fluffy *poori* breads are used to scoop up spicy fresh vegetable specialties made from ingredients such as beans, eggplant, okra tomatoes, and potatoes. The Gujarati *thaali* is traditionally a large stainless steel plate containing four to six small round bowls, each filled with a different vegetarian delicacy. On the side, fresh, hot *rotlis* (flatbreads), rice, pickles, and chutneys are served as accompaniments. This collection of over 80 family recipes introduces readers to some of India's often overlooked culinary offerings.

Also included are an introduction to Gujarati culture and cuisine, section on spices, ingredients, and utensils, and a chapter on non-vegetarian specialties. Each recipe is presented in an easy-to-follow format and adapted for the North American kitchen. Enchanting drawings throughout the book bring the flavors of India alive.

Two-Color • 180 pages • 6 x 9 • $22.50hc • 0-7818-1060-4 • W • (92)

Healthy South Indian Cooking

Alamelu Vairavan & Patricia Marquardt

With an emphasis on the famed Chettinad cooking tradition of southern India, these 197 recipes, mostly vegetarian, will allow home cooks to create exotic fare such as Masala Dosa, Pearl Onion and Tomato Sambhar, and Eggplant Masala Curry. Each of these low-fat, low-calorie recipes includes complete nutritional anaylsis. Also included are sample menus of complementary dishes, as well as innovative suggestions for integrating South Indian dishes into Western meals. A multilingual glossary of spices and ingredients, a section on the preparation of dals (a staple lentil dish), and 16 pages of color photographs make this book a clear and concise introduction to the healthy, delicious cooking of South India.

350 pages • 5½ x 8½ • 16-page color photo insert • 0-7818-0867-7 • $24.95pb • (69)

HISTORY & CULTURE

India: An Illustrated History

Prem Kishore & Anuradha Kishore Ganpati

This succinct volume recounts 45,000 years of Indian history, from the earlist settlements of the Indus Valley through the twentieth-century struggle against British imperial rule. It concludes with a recounting of the challenges facing the country today. Sections on dress, regional cuisine, and cultural traditions being the various aspects of this diverse nation to life.

234 pages • 5 x 7 • 50 photos/illus/maps • 0-7818-0944-4 • $14.95pb • (424)

Treasury of Indian Love

Poems & Proverbs from the Indian Sub-Continent

Edited by Christopher Shackle and Nicholas Awde

This collection features over 100 love poems and proverbs in the original Indian languages, side-by-side with translations into English. Included are works from 37 separate languages, among them Sanskrit, Assamese, Bengali, Gujarati, Hindi, Kannada, Kashmiri, Mayalayam, Marathi, Punjabi, Rajasthani, Tamil, and Urdu.

228 pages • 5 x 7 • 0-7818-0670-4 • $11.95hc • (768)

LANGUAGE

Hindi Children's Picture Dictionary
English-Hindi/Hindi-English
Full-Color • 625 entries • 500 illustrations • 104 pages • 8½ x 11 • 0-7818-1129-5 • $14.95pb • (319) • Available in the Summer of 2006

Hindi-English/English-Hindi Practical Dictionary
25,000 entries • 745 pages • 4½ x 7 • 0-7818-0084-6 • $19.95pb • (442)

Hindi-English/English-Hindi Standard Dictionary
30,000 entries • 800 pages • 6 x 9 • 0-7818-0470-1 • $27.50pb • (559)

Teach Yourself Hindi
207 pages • $4^3/_8$ x 7 • 0-87052-831-9 • $11.95pb • (170)

Teach Yourself Marathi
144 pages • 5½ x 8½ • 0-87052-620-0 • $9.95pb • (278)

Punjabi-English/English-Punjabi Dictionary
25,000 entries • 782 pages • 5 x 7 • 0-7818-0940-1 • $19.95pb • (401)

Sanskrit-English Concise Dictionary
18,000 pages • 380 pages • 4 x 6 • 0-7818-0203-2 • $14.95pb • (605)

Sanskrit Grammar for Beginners
324 pages • 5½ x 8½ • 0-7818-1075-2 • $17.95pb • (135)

Tamil-English/English-Tamil Dictionary & Phrasebook
6,000 entries • 250 pages • 3¾ x 7½ • 0-7818-1016-7 • $12.95pb • (81)